DESIGNING THE SERMON

Abingdon Preacher's Library

Liberation Preaching, Justo L. and Catherine G. González
The Person in the Pulpit, Willard F. Jabusch
The Preaching Moment, Charles L. Bartow
Designing the Sermon, James Earl Massey
The Preaching Tradition, DeWitte T. Holland
The Sermon as God's Word, Robert W. Duke
Creative Preaching, Elizabeth Achtemeier
The Word in Worship, William Skudlarek
Preaching as Communication, Myron R. Chartier
A Theology of Preaching, Richard Lischer
Preaching Biblically, William D. Thompson
Integrative Preaching, William H. Willimon

DESIGNING
THE SERMON
·
Order and Movement in Preaching

James Earl Massey

ABINGDON PREACHER'S LIBRARY

William D. Thompson, Editor

ABINGDON PRESS
Nashville

DESIGNING THE SERMON: ORDER AND MOVEMENT IN PREACHING

Library of Congress Cataloging in Publication Data

MASSEY, JAMES EARL.
 Designing the sermon.
 (Abingdon preacher's library series)
 Bibliography: p.
 Includes index.
 1. Preaching. I.   Title.
BV4211.2.M277   251   80-17920

ISBN 0-687-10490-4

Scripture quotations unless otherwise noted are from the Revised Standard Version Common Bible, copyrighted © 1973 by the Division of Christian Education of the National Council of Churches of Christ in the U.S.A., and are used by permission.

The author's sermons "Anatomy of a Failure," "He Was Faithful," and "Death Did Not Win!" in chapter 7 originally appeared in *Vital Christianity*, in the issues, respectively, of May 13, 1979; September 23, 1979; and April 8, 1979. They are used here by permission of Warner Press, Inc.

MANUFACTURED BY THE PARTHENON PRESS AT
NASHVILLE, TENNESSEE, UNITED STATES OF AMERICA

To
Two Senior Statesmen in the Spirit
JOHN MALCUS ELLISON
(1889-1979)
and
HOWARD THURMAN
with appreciation
for counsel,
encouragement,
and
exemplary ministries

CONTENTS

EDITOR'S FOREWORD   9

PREFACE   11

I. THE SERMON IN CONTEXT   15
Preaching and Reality—Preaching Goals and Sermon Design—An Overview of Basic Sermon Forms—Some Contemporary Concerns in Sermon Design—Toward Adequacy in Designing a Sermon—The "Why" of It All

II. DESIGNING THE NARRATIVE/STORY SERMON   35
Story as a Primary Mode in Scripture—Story-Preaching in the Black Church Tradition—The Present Tense in Story-Life—"Story" in the Preaching of Jesus—Readying the Narrative Sermon—A Stubborn Fact and Faith

III. DESIGNING THE TEXTUAL/EXPOSITORY SERMON   50
Some Guidelines and Examples—The Lure of the Ideal

IV. DESIGNING THE DOCTRINAL/TOPICAL SERMON   61
The New Testament Focus on Doctrine—Doctrine: Faith's Ground Plan—The Doctrinal Sermon—Beyond Teaching to Assurance and Action

V. DESIGNING THE FUNERAL SERMON   75
The Ritual Context of Funerals—Some Guidelines for the Funeral Sermon Design

VI. STUDYING THE METHODS OF MASTER
    PREACHERS   83
    Theorizing from Life—From One Preacher to Another—A
    Few Cautions—Guidelines for Studying Sermons—The
    Basic Objective Reviewed

VII. THREE ILLUSTRATED DESIGNS   97
    Sermon Style 1. Narrative/Story: "Anatomy of a Fail-
    ure"—Sermon Style 2. Textual/Expository: "He Was
    Faithful"—Sermon Style 3. Doctrinal/Topical: "Death Did
    Not Win!"

    NOTES   113

    FOR FURTHER READING   121

    INDEX   125

EDITOR'S FOREWORD

Preaching has captured the attention of increasingly large segments of the American public. Lay parish committees seeking pastoral leadership consistently rank preaching as the most desirable pastoral skill. Seminary courses and clergy conferences on preaching attract participants in larger numbers than ever. Millions of viewers watch television preachers every week.

What is *good* preaching? is the question of both those who hear it and those who do it. Hearers answer that question instinctively, tuning in the preacher who meets their needs, whether in the pulpit of the neighborhood church or on a broadcast. Preachers need to answer more intentionally.

Time was that a good thick book on preaching would do it, or a miscellaneous smattering of thin ones. The time now seems ripe for a different kind of resource—a carefully conceived, tightly edited series of books whose scope covers the homiletical spectrum and whose individual volumes reveal the latest and best thinking about each specialty within the field of preaching. The volumes in the Abingdon Preacher's Library enable the preacher to understand preaching in its historical setting; to examine its biblical and theological underpinnings; to explore its spiritual, relational, and liturgical dimensions; and to develop insights into its craftsmanship.

Designed primarily for use in the seminary classroom, this series will also serve the practicing preacher whose background in homiletics is spotty or out-of-date, or whose preaching needs strengthening in some specific area.

William D. Thompson
Eastern Baptist Theological Seminary
Philadelphia, Pennsylvania

PREFACE

The present study was written, like the other books in the Abingdon Preacher's Library series, with two groups of readers in view: seminarians in need of current and supplemental helps for designing and developing sermons, and working ministers on the hunt for suggestions and guidance by which to sharpen their skills for pulpit work. This fact will help to explain both the sometimes heavy documentation that fills the Notes section at the end, and the almost totally nontechnical writing that fills these pages.

This study centers attention upon sermon design, with special focus on order and movement. While there are many other books that treat the formal and functional elements of sermon preparation, this one supplements such basic guidance through its guidelines for a more contemporary approach in shaping specific classifications of sermon types. This book differs further in that its guidelines are copiously illustrated not only in these pages but in conjunction with a resource book of sermons: *The Twentieth Century Pulpit*, edited by James W. Cox (Nashville: Abingdon, 1978). Considerable reference has been made also to the multivolumed set: *Twenty Centuries of Great Preaching: An Encyclopedia of Preaching*, edited by Clyde E. Fant, Jr., and William M. Pinson, Jr. (Waco, Texas: Word Books, 1971). In addition to this, suggestions for still further reading are listed at the end of the book.

The reader might reason that a seemingly disproportionate amount of discussion has been given to narrative/story sermons as compared with the shorter treatment accorded the other types categorized in this book. The explanation for this is simple. Textual, expository, doctrinal, and topical concerns have been given extensive coverage across many decades and in many, many books, but story preaching is just beginning to gain due recognition in formal circles of critical discussion. There remains a scarcity of work on the story sermon design, and at the very time people and preachers are showing increased interest in it.

There were several possibilities to choose from in treating the "occasional" kind of sermon. I chose to deal with designing a funeral sermon. The reasoning behind this will be readily apparent to most readers.

William D. Thompson, general editor of this Abingdon Preacher's Library series, graciously shared suggestions, critical counsel, and prompt prodding as this writing was underway. I am deeply indebted to him for the opportunity to share in making one of the volumes in this timely series of helps for preachers.

I took the liberty—and the risk—of including three of my own sermons as illustrative instances of specific design possibilities. Placed last, as chapter 7, the three sermons may be examined as one preacher's approach to using the respective sermon design guidelines offered in this book. Each sermon has been tested, and by wide use—on the weekly international radio program "The Christian Brotherhood Hour," in connection with my denominational assignment as its radio preacher. I do not offer these three sermons as exemplary (as worth imitating), but as examples (samples, illustrations).

A. N. Sherwin-White, about to rehearse some old facts for

readers in his then newest book, began with a tongue-in-cheek apology to some who might view his restatement as "old hat." He explained, "You are bound to say from time to time 'we have heard this before,' though perhaps you will not always say 'we have heard *all* this before.' I hope to put a new shine on some of the old lamps."[1]

That is my interest and prayer in sending forth these pages. *Soli Deo Gloria.*

JAMES EARL MASSEY

Anderson Graduate School of Theology

I. THE SERMON IN CONTEXT

"The real preacher," Walter Russell Bowie remarked, "is more than a maker of sermons. He is a medium of contact between God and the minds and hearts of men."[1] Bowie was placing both preacher and sermon in context, calling attention to what makes the preacher strategic and what makes the sermon important. At the heart of the preacher's work must be a clear understanding that sermons are part of a larger statement and that those who design and deliver them must partake of a larger Life.

PREACHING AND REALITY

Bowie's words place an accent on "the real preacher" as one who draws vitality from God and shares it with others by what is preached. Real preaching will therefore have a definite ring to it and a distinct power in it. Real preaching will not allow for sermons that are abstract, arrogantly eloquent, or terrifyingly out of touch with life and God.

Real preaching is rooted in God's concern for persons. The basic message of Scripture is about a real God who seeks our good. Jesus had a lot to say about God's concern, his nearness, and his deeds. Jesus did not speak of God as an ideal or as a regulating idea but as Father, concerned about the human family and active in our world.

W. R. Inge once explained that "God is a fact, not an ideal."[2] Preaching lives in the light of God as the first of all facts, and it heralds the truth that God *is* and that "he rewards those who seek him" (Heb. 11:6b). These are root matters by which real preaching lives. By such preaching, hearers are helped in gaining a proper worldview and selfview. By such preaching, hearers are affirmed, undergirded for life—whatever its paradoxes, tragedies, distresses, distortions.

Real preaching is an agency of the grace of God. The sermon therefore deals with what does not originate with us; it discloses and describes and invites, offering something more to hearers than a mere theological statement. Drawing from the larger statement about God's concern and grace, the sermon is designed and preached to "open men upwards," so that the reality of God's graciousness will affect all who hear, and at those levels where real needs are most acutely known.

It must be said, and with emphasis: real preaching is not merely concerned with the nature of religious experience; it helps the hearer to experience grace, that divine help which deals with human sin and crippling experiences. As Helmut Thielicke has rightly explained, real preaching involves helping hearers "meet the decisive, active Word," that "strikes us as an effectual Word . . . [which] breaks off the old existence and starts a new one, bringing sins to light and forgiving them, changing God's rejection into an acceptance which gives me a new future and makes me a new creature in the miracle of the Spirit."[3]

It is not incidental that there are so many narratives about sin in our Bible. Nor is it accidental. Sin has been, and continues to be, the human reality. But where sin abounded, grace abounds all the more (Rom. 5:20).

Real preaching will highlight what Scripture gladly reports:

that there is mercy to match any misery, and grace to handle any guilt. None who study the Bible aright can miss the clear notice there of the "sin-grace dialectic."[4] Interestingly, our knowledge of sin deepens as we learn more about grace, but that same message opens to us the way out of guilt and shame. Real preaching will always bear this double character and wield this double power, all of which is of "a radical consequence for the structure of preaching."[5] We see ourselves truly only when under the light of grace. And it is by that light that our change can come and our needed help be received.

Real preaching therefore takes seriously the moral and spiritual climate of the times. It does not assume that proclaiming biblical statements is adequate, neglecting to probe and address those prevailing assumptions and beliefs which have determined the major problems of our times. The real preacher will seek to know just what dominates the thought life of those who hear the sermons, and will want to understand the loyalties to which the energies and time of the people are being given.

Our generation stands lost in a wilderness of secularity, relativism, proneness to question, and the loss of any felt need to be accountable. The judgment of sinful, selfish living weighs heavily upon life in our time, and the evidences of a diseased human condition continue to suggest the need for help from beyond ourselves.

Preaching both points to that help and brings it within reach. The sermon shines best when the skies are dark and wrong choices burden people with a heavy awareness of failure and loss. So we design our sermons and preach them—not to preserve a world or to protect it, but to create a new order through announcing hope for change and bidding all to accept and act upon that hope and need.

It is in this light that such texts as Romans 10:14-15 and I Corinthians 1:21 must be viewed. These verses make it abundantly clear that God's will and way stand so stoutly

revealed through preaching that something would be missed in
the world if preaching had not called attention to it. That
something is divine grace, grace offered by the One who makes
preaching breathe his concern and evidence his presence.

Preaching must be real to be vital. It must deal with real
people with real needs, offering needed help from a real God. It
must proceed according to realistic goals: informing, persuading, encouraging, reminding, sustaining, and *giving* as it moves
toward those goals.

PREACHING GOALS AND SERMON DESIGN

The ultimate goal in preaching is to connect the hearer with
the grace of God, and nurture that hearer in the life that grace
makes possible when it is accepted and regarded in full. Nothing
less than this basic objective is worthy of any pulpit, and nothing
other than this concern can rightly qualify as Christian
preaching. Christian preaching is always rooted in the purpose
Jesus announced for his coming: "I come that they may have
life, and have it abundantly" (John 10:10). A preaching ministry
maintains focus and balance when that purpose of Christ is kept
central in all sermon planning.

But there are immediate goals for specific sermons, and these
determine the focus and design of individual sermons at a given
time. A sermon can be preached to offer a solution to a problem,
or to instruct in an essential doctrine, or to prescribe a cure for
some spiritual or social ill; it can be planned to support a cause,
or to sustain hearers and keep them "on their feet" while living
under pressure. In each instance of focus the preacher should be
concerned with being understood, effective, and successful in
securing the intended response from those who hear the
sermon. The particular purpose of each sermon should be
reflected in a design planned with that response in view.

Those who preach must develop a basic orientation to the

need for *sermon design*. This will keep the preacher process-oriented as the pulpit work is projected and planned. Any sermon worth hearing will grow out of a heart and head whose feeling and thought have been projected toward some clear end to which the speaking will move.

Biologist C. M. Child once wrote: "Structure and function are mutually related. Function produces structure and structure modifies and determines the character of function." All of which is to say that *design is related to what one intends to do.*

Speaking about what one intends to do by preaching, there is that useful story W. E. Sangster delighted in telling about a certain seminary student and his defective sermon. [6] The student had preached in class before his fellow students and the professor. It was something of an omen if the student was afterward asked by the professor to come to the office and bring the manuscript of the sermon along for discussion. That student was so asked, and he went in to see the professor. He placed his sermon manuscript down on the teacher's desk and sat down beside the desk in silent horror. The professor sat in silence too, studying the sermon sheets. Finally the student broke the silence, pleading anxiously, "It will do, Sir, won't it? It will do?" To which the professor displeasingly replied, "Do *what?*"

It was with the need to keep the sermon focused on a goal that Sangster reminded us, "Preaching is meant to do things." There are specific responses we seek in preaching, and if we are to achieve a determined end, we must design the sermon with that response or end in view. The design is to structure the sermon message, yes, but more centrally to relate that message to the hearer's life, touching intellect and emotions both, prodding thought and feeling and essential action. A timely, properly planned sermon can help effect this end.

"Design" can be a noun, indicating a product or a form. It can be a verb, indicating a process or function. But whether it is seen as product or process, behind the one or the other stands the designer, someone working with an end in view and a plan by which to reach it. The preacher must be a designer to achieve the goals of the gospel and handle the preaching task with some growing competence.

This means that the sermon design should have a clear aim and logical structure. The sermon idea or theme should be outlined in a reasonable sequence, the materials so organized and arranged that a buildup is achieved in the hearer's understanding and feelings, so that a climax of impression results and the time of hearing will lead to definite action in faith and life. The sermon design is therefore ordered for the sake of an experience; it is planned to make the hearing a "happening." The design should have focus, balance, logical sequence, emphasis, supportive detail, strategic illustrative support, and calculated impact through a climax of impression.[7]

An effective design will have a point to make, an idea to express, a scene to share, a cause to promote, a doctrine to set forth and apply, an action to inspire, a feeling to arouse, a direction to point out, a divine promise to share, a caution to give, a person to claim. Design is vital in sermon planning and delivery.[8]

AN OVERVIEW OF BASIC SERMON FORMS

The situational nature of the sermon has always allowed the widest latitude for handling its structure, arrangement, and design. Although the most appropriate design begins with the preacher asking the question of what the sermon should be planned to achieve, the final details of that planning can be as individual as the occasion for the sermon and the preacher who must address the persons involved as hearers in it. Having admitted this, it is nevertheless necessary to say that in the long history of Christian preaching certain basic forms of sermonizing have been isolated and regarded as modular.

1. The most popular and traditional sermon form is the *topical* (or subject). This design highlights the truth or importance of a topic or theme, letting the logical points or facets of that topic control the sequence of treatment and timing of the application. The topic can be chosen from any one of a number of sources, but it is usually backed or supported by a related scriptural text. The topic might be a phrase ("The Prodigal Son"), or a sentence ("The Sacred and the Secular Are Inseparable,"), a question ("And How Does It All End?"), or even just one word ("Easter"),[9] but in each instance the subject or topic provides the source of focus and control. The treatment derives from the logical order suggested by the topic the preacher chose.

The topical or subject sermon continues to maintain its popularity because of the obvious benefits this design allows. It is not incidental that "in the history of preaching, topical sermons have outnumbered all the rest."[10] Together with an obviously wider range of variety of topics to choose and use, this design also allows for the most innovation on the preacher's part: the number of "points" in the structure is not necessarily restricted or predetermined; one can be doctrinal, devotional, evangelistic, meditational, and so on; the preacher's own personal bent can find freedom; and the ability to achieve and maintain unity is helped by a determining topic. These are some of the main reasons for the popularity of the topical or subject sermon form.

2. The second-most-used sermon form is the *textual*, a form of design determined mainly by the divisions or sequences of thought in a single text or short passage from Scripture. Although it is possible to treat a text topically, creating a blend traditionally labeled textual-topical, the scales are usually tipped to the textual side or to the topical thrust. In most cases where a blend is sought, both the text and the topic are reflected in the sermon structure and sequence of arrangement.

An excellent example of a purely textual sermon is Karl Barth's "Look Up to Him!" based on Psalm 34:5. This sermon, delivered to prisoners on or near Ascension Day, took its outline and progression and subject from the text itself, with two main points:[11]

    I. Look up to Him—Jesus Christ, our Savior
   II. The results of looking:
        a) momentous change in us through Christ
        b) the release from shame and fear before God

The design is simple and straightforward. "Homiletical fundamentalist" as he was, Barth combined application with the making of his statement; the biblical word was itself seen as the relevant issue, so that additional interest-gathering factors were not sought nor applied. "He believed that when God's revelation is proclaimed to men it gathers its own interest and makes its own applications, and no further illustration or application is needed or proper in Christian preaching."[12]

Referring again to the research volume of contemporary models, "The Doctrine of the Trinity" by Donald M. Baillie is a clear and forceful example of a textual-topical sermon.[13] The sermon form and focus are influenced by both the text (Matt. 28:19—"In the name of the Father, and of the Son, and of the Holy Ghost") and the topic.

3. A third sermon form is the *expositional*, the design of which is determined basically by an extended passage of Scripture. In true exposition the thought and treatment are controlled by the textual passage. "God's Inescapable Nearness" by Eduard Schweizer is basically expositional in form.[14] Based on Philippians 4:4-8, most of the biblical base is covered in the treatment the preacher has given.

Most teachers of homiletics agree that an expository sermon has *predetermined matter* to be presented, namely a biblical text or passage or book, but not all agree on the variety possible in the *manner* of treatment. The exposition should be influenced by the nature of genre of the passage to be treated, and when one observes this rule, then the manner of treatment will necessarily vary from sermon to sermon. A passage from Romans, for example, might be explanatory—chapter 6 is a primary instance—so the treatment should conform to the style, tone, and thrust of the teaching presented there. A passage can be argumentative, as I Corinthians 15, so the exposition should deal with the point the Apostle Paul wrote to settle a controversy. A biblical passage might be a narrative, or a dialogue, in which instance the manner of treatment might well take a different turn from the direction other writing forms dictate. In any case, the expositional sermon will center attention upon some one emphasis in a text or passage, purposefully treating a teaching, an insight, a promise, a hope, a warning, a character, an experience, a meaning, a prophecy, a virtue, a key word, and so on. But whatever the length of the passage, and whatever the style of the source, the expositional manner can have variety and value when it remains focused, interesting, and life-oriented. The best exposition draws attention to the light that is in the Word of God, while at the same time calling attention to the human situation and promise of hope because of that light. When this balance is maintained, the exposition will always serve human experience, meeting human needs rather than merely centering on a passage. Like all good preaching, exposition must be designed and delivered to make hearers understand, feel, and act.

The three basic classifications of sermon forms discussed above are traditional in the history of homiletics. There are other ways to classify sermon types. W. E. Sangster, in his *Craft of Sermon Construction*, has treated sermons along three lines of difference: their subject matter (content), their structural type (arrangement or design), and their psychological method (how the preacher seeks to "put it over").[15] However classified, sermonic elements do tend to overlap, making for mixed types more often than not. "The ideal sermon will be as biblical in content and as functional in meeting a definite need as possible."[16]

SOME CONTEMPORARY CONCERNS IN SERMON DESIGN

The sermon forms and styles discussed above all have behind them the considerable weight of long use and proven adequacy. Although there are those preachers who continue to show that the old established forms still breathe in vital fashion, many voices are being raised advising that the old forms and approaches need to be adapted in the interest of greater variety and wider public appeal. There is much to be said for increased appeal and the need to move beyond the limitations of stilted stereotypes—and I am about to treat some of what is being said and suggested—but when I hear discussions about some sermon form being outmoded I recall something musician Richard Wagner reportedly remarked upon hearing Johannes Brahms play his scintillating Variations and Fugue on a Theme by Handel. Although Wagner was not especially fond of Brahms, he was so moved by the composer's genius that he declared, "That shows what may still be done with the old forms provided someone appears who knows how to treat them."

The old forms are not necessarily obsolete. The need is for preachers who are willing to work at better ways of treating and using them. The following approaches address that concern.

1. *Increased Understanding of the Listener.* This approach to preaching seeks to harness insights from communication theory about the dynamics at work in the communication process— that is, how and why any hearer listens, what gains and benefits are promised by the speaker, what is necessary to secure the hearer's response, and so forth.

This listener-approach to preaching seeks to relate scientific method and scriptural insight to personal needs. It seeks to balance technique with truth, all in the hearer's interest. There are two principles involved in this approach: the principle of interest and the principle of involvement. Interest has to do with the way the preacher matches the message to the listener's world of personal concerns, while involvement relates to the interaction and agreement the preacher elicits by what is said and heard. We all know that the greater the sense of relation between speaker and hearer, the more immediate and effective the communication process becomes.[17]

Any sermon will have increased appeal when an increased understanding of the listener and his or her personal world informs the planning behind it. When one seriously regards the basic psychology at work in the hearer during the listening moment, it is far more likely that the hearer will open the doors of perception to what is being said. Addressing the hearer's self-awareness in the light of his or her life-awareness usually encourages interest to listen and become involved in the issues of the listening event.

Although so much more can be said about this approach, it will suffice to add but one more facet at this point. So much of what can happen toward interesting and involving the hearer lies with the preacher: how the preacher is willing to work at developing skills in using words, depth of knowledge, nurturing an attitude of obvious caring, and the willingness to share the fullness of "soul" in the speaking of any statement.

James Black wrote many years ago, "Behind all preaching, during our preparation in the study or in the execution itself, there should be *the shadow of a listening people*. . . . The form, tone, and colour of preaching are definitely prescribed by this fact."[18]

The design of any sermon must have in it a sense of the hearer. This goes beyond the careful handling of a subject, and even beyond the psychology of an audience as such.

2. *Increased Regard for the Worship Context.* Although this regard for the worship context of the sermon is not really new, there is a new wave of concern these days to relate the sermon more dynamically to other elements in the experience of worship. In some groups where preaching once fell under the shadow of the Mass or Holy Eucharist, there is an increased concern to highlight its importance as itself a sacrament. One can read about this concern, for example, in the Roman Catholic Church's *Constitution on the Sacred Liturgy,* a theological document that grew out of the proceedings of the Second Vatican Council of 1962-64. A reading of Articles 35 and 52 of that document will show that the sermon in that church's life is being regarded now as something more than an interlude in the liturgy, that it is now being highlighted more and more as a serious statement about the Word and how that Word relates to the hearer's life as a means of grace.[19]

The same concern to relate the sermon more dynamically to the worship setting is also evident in churches less liturgy-centered. More and more preachers are finding increased guidance for sermonic thrust in a depth study of the cycle and emphases of the church year. Helped by such directions, the alert preacher can more readily relate texts and topics and themes to the worship setting. The dynamism of this approach is apparent in the extensive use allowed for scripture in the service through the lectionary, with the preacher as interpreter of the texts, applying their meanings to life and the listener's situated needs.

Merrill R. Abbey has helpfully explained:

> The Christian message is not seasonal, but the seasons help to hold to the light the varied facets of its one jewel. Underlying each season is an aspect of the gospel which—though not confined to a season—focuses attention during one period upon an element in the Christian faith and life which cannot be lost if the total message is to be truly heard.[20]

Abbey has called attention to the ways a fuller understanding of the Christian faith is assisted by a lectionary. Not only is the worshiper helped to enter more fully into the Christian interpretation of life, but the preacher's artful work is deepened in at least three dimensions: biblical-exegetical, prophetic-practical, and liturgical. And viewed from the perspective of the total worship setting, this helps to reduce the limiting subjectivism that could afflict the preacher's arbitrary choices of texts and themes. There is great help toward better preaching through the "strong key passages" afforded in a well-ordered lectionary, and the worship service so ordered provides for many a more enriched circle of meaning out of which to believe and live.

Viewed in this way, the planning behind a sermon is influenced by the stated textual passage(s) of a given day and the meaning of the occasion when it will be heard. What identifies the day in its relation to the church's teaching schedule also gives the preacher his sermon direction and proper focus, and sometimes a suggested form. Such preaching honors the meaning of the church, the progression of the church in history, the need to relate each generation with that meaning and progression; it aids recall, assists renewal, and has been germane in the spiritual formation of those who have been heirs of that tradition.

3. *The Shaping of Community Through Preaching.* This third contemporary concern which has influenced the work of sermon designing is closely related to the second treated above. Again, this is not a new concern, but there has been an increased regard for it in our time.

Dietrich Bonhoeffer (1906–1945), preoccupied with the nature and meaning and work of the church across his busy but brief life, had a lot to say about this in his doctoral dissertation, *The Communion of Saints,* his first major work.[21] Although in that work he was grappling with a sociological understanding of the church and its theology, he described preaching as essentially related to its life. "Preaching is the 'ministry' of the church, so there must also be a congregation. The one implies the other. . . . Preaching is an activity of the church divinely ordained for the church." All of which is true, he added, even when the believer risks "having to face a narrow-minded preacher alongside spiritless faces."[22] But despite any and all "unedifying factors," as Bonhoeffer termed them, the preached word is a means for community.

More recently James M. Gustafson has written: "The preacher's function is to bring a particular people into a more significant relation to the meanings of the Church. . . . He views a concrete human community in the light of the truths to which the total Christian community adheres."[23]

The time and place in which this most regularly occurs is the time and place of congregational worship. The setting, the meaning, the scriptures, the sharing, and the sermon all interact; but it is the preaching that declares those meanings in contemporary fashion, extends those meanings to a given people, and applies those meanings so as to elicit faith and sustain a people during their procession and mission.

This approach to preaching influences the preacher to work always for a strengthened community spirit among his hearers by assisting their worship and work. The preacher's concern embraces every individual member, but that concern links the individual hearer with the wider group for fellowship, worship, and work as a community of faith.

4. *Increased Attention to the Narrative Mode in Scripture and the Story Quality of Human Life.* One of the most signal trends now under study by homileticians is the return to a major use of narrative, both as source and style for theology and preaching. With novelists sifting the narrative quality of human life, and writing in depth about the meaning of movement in our thought and planning, theologians are also busy sifting Scripture and

history and events for perspective and discernible patterns of meaning.[24] Narrative is an ancient, popular, and dynamic way of organizing, preserving, and presenting the meanings in life; reality is readily sensed through the telling of a story. Narratives excite interest and prod involvement by way of identification.

Narrative, or "story," has an immediate advantage over argument, as its popularity and interest-pulling qualities prove beyond any doubt. Story is hardly ever dry and dull; it is usually dynamic. Henry H. Mitchell has recently suggested, and with great warrant, that the true recovery of preaching as a powerful theological solution will not happen through more analysis and discursive rhetoric but through meaningful, celebrative, folk-level, dialogical, biblical story-telling.[25]

Story communicates with the whole person. It reaches more sectors of the self than just the rational. "People comprehend pictorially what they cannot comprehend conceptually," Mitchell explains. Well narrated action always produces a dominant impression on a hearer's mind and spirit—and emotional zone. There are considerable riches for the preaching task in the narrative mode in Scripture, the story quality in human life, and story features and style of presentation in a sermon design.

5. *The Message Organization Approach.* Given the factors stated above—an increased understanding of the listener's stake in the communication process, an increased regard for the worship setting in which preaching occurs, the need to shape and sustain the church through preaching, and the importance of "story" for meaning and methodology, then the basic planning to shape a proper sermon design matters supremely.

The topic of the message, its textual base, the logical progression of the unfolding thought, proper illustrative matter, and the timing of each sequence—all these are involved in what must be organized or "arranged" by the preacher in shaping a sermon. An adequate arrangement of the aspects and levels in a message helps the preacher to handle it and the hearer to understand it. The attitude of interest or indifference on the listener's part is significantly affected by how the message is introduced, and the involvement that message demands is more likely to happen if its "points" or aspects are well-illustrated and duly emphasized for appropriate impact. Transition in the message needs to be timely, and all movement must be toward a clear goal or purpose.

The challenge of a message can be guaranteed, but the acceptance of a message is always conditional. A well-designed sermon can always challenge, making its impact in the hearer's consciousness, but the verdict and vote about acting positively and readily on that message rests finally with the hearer, not with the preacher who issues the challenge. Meanwhile the basic ingredients to assist understanding and persuasion rest with the preacher, and the organization of the sermon is crucial to it all.

TOWARD ADEQUACY IN DESIGNING A SERMON

Some guiding principles now follow for shaping a sermon plan and procedure. The principles suggested here are general and apply to most sermons, while additional and specific guidance about certain classified sermon forms will be set forth in the chapters that will treat them.

1. *A communicative design must begin with some one idea that focuses on a human issue or divine claim.* In either case a *need* is in the foreground—some human condition to which one must speak or some divine concern to which one must point the hearer's attention.

The "idea" is the message-germ. It can come to the preacher's attention in any one of a number of ways: from something read, from counseling experiences, from some visit, from a knowledge of congregational needs, from close study of the

Bible, from an insight during the time of prayer, from a suggestion by a member or friend—in short, from one's coming and going and the perennial round of human concerns and needs.

The idea is what generates thoughtfulness, and out of that thoughtfulness grows the sermon. The sermon is the development of a theme growing out of an idea that focuses on a human issue or divine claim. The idea is the germ of the message, the theme forecasts the direction of the message, and the sermon is the full plan to address and involve the hearer in the idea.

2. *Give the idea authoritative focus by the support of a scripture verse or passage.* Every sermon is stronger when its central idea is rooted in the Word, when its thrust is clearly allied with the authority of revelation.

If the basic sermon idea has grown out of the text, that is better still because the layout and focus of the text can direct the preacher in structuring the sermon design. Most texts and passages can be separated quite logically into natural divisions of thought, and these divisions will suggest the structure and movement essential to the sermon.

The text or passage should be studied with care, read and re-read in context, so that background factors are clearly seen and its central focus *deeply felt* as well as understood. Much needs to be said about the importance of living with a text until its inner message grips the preacher. This being gripped means to have gone beyond the technical issues of studying the text and to have felt the tensions of the truth that text presents. The best designs grow out of an inward seeing and a depth of feeling. Pianist Clifford Curzon tells about his celebrated teacher Artur Schnabel cautioning his piano students: " 'Play nothing before you hear it'—or, 'First hear, then play.' He knew that only certainty of conception could produce clarity of presentation." And it is so in mining a text for its meaning and message.

3. *Begin structuring the textual message or topical theme.* The most fruitful issue of clear thought about the text or theme is the

ability to condense its insight into a full sentence. The single sentence will help greatly in opening logical direction for treating the message.

The structure should be natural and unforced. If a theme is your guide, then organize your treatment of it with supportive and sequential logic. If a text is your guide, then follow its lead and let its vibrations be felt at every point in your planning. As T. L. Cuyler once advised, "The sap of the text should reach the farthest twig of the sermon."[26]

The sermon structure must have essential unity in all its parts and "points." Although the whole is greater than the sum of its parts, the parts and points relate significantly to that wholeness—but under strict conditions: a natural and unforced outline, a theme or text that is central and controlling, and a sequential movement that has a good start and a worthy goal.

The sermon structure must have logical proportion in the way its central idea is featured. Stress and balance are crucial to this end, so the preacher should plan to move along from the simplest level of the idea to its more complex features, pacing it all to achieve unmistakable clarity and impact.

The sermon idea must be clearly illustrated as each sequence occurs in its unfolding. As for that sequence, transitional sentences are a must. Sequential movement in the sermon is helped when each point or progression in thought actually gives a new angle of vision into the message. Clearly related transitional sentences can motivate the hearer to anticipate the change and accept it as natural and timely. As for the number of points or levels of thought to be treated in a message, that should be dictated by the text, the topic, the time of hearing, and good taste. Tradition might also give some guidance about this.

4. *The final focus of the sermon is application of the idea or insight to the hearer's life.* Although it is possible and helpful to make preliminary application of a textual message as one proceeds in sequence to unfold it—as did Karl Barth in his

message "Look Up to Him!"[27]—there is a greater depth of involvement sought and expected in connection with the conclusion of a message. While the introduction to the sermon has to secure the hearer's interest, the conclusion of the sermon has to prod the hearer into action—and it is the preacher's last moment to do so. The central statement has been made as the message unfolded. The insight has been illustrated and made clear. Now, in the concluding words, decision is demanded and action urged. The sermon that ends without celebration stirred or personal challenge felt will have made little difference for having been heard.

5. *So: Write the sermon out after giving time and thought about its structure and goal.* The writing is not to shape a literary product but to express a living, dynamic statement. Writing will help to ensure a high quality of organization, motivated sequence, and strategic control of the material and message.

The sermon is an oral presentation, to be sure, but careful writing of it helps us see in fact what we want to say in faith. Writing lets us see the relations between the theme and how we treat it, how we balance statements and illustrations of their meaning, how we move between objective fact and subjective expression. Writing the sermon out in full helps us control the stylistic levels necessary for the widest public appeal. In reviewing a written sermon, the preacher can check for punning, understatement, overstatement, tasteful expressions, clarity of objective, vocabulary, and mental tone. Writing the sermon helps the preacher catch the hearer's ear, because the sermon is so designed and aimed. Writing the sermon helps to time the flow of words, thus assisting not only an exactness but an economy of expression.

THE "WHY" OF IT ALL

Charles Haddon Spurgeon (1834–1892), whose pulpit ministry and sermonic prowess were universally applauded, both showed and taught his ministerial students in the Pastors' College the principles of preaching, and in exemplary fashion. Talking about sermons in one of his Friday lectures to the seminarians, Spurgeon advised: "We do not enter the pulpit to talk for talk's sake; we have instructions to convey important to the last degree, and we cannot afford to utter pretty nothings. . . . The true minister of Christ knows that the true value of a sermon must lie, not in its fashion and manner, but in the truth it contains."[28]

The best perspective on a sermon is to see it in the light of its purpose under God. And those who truly see that purpose will live and work to keep their efforts in the study and the pulpit always within that context. Again, Spurgeon: "set no store by the quantity of words which you utter, but strive to be esteemed for the quality of your matter."

II. DESIGNING THE
NARRATIVE/STORY SERMON

One does not need to read very far in the Bible to discover the story-power that fills its pages, and the preacher who stays open to the narratives and stories reported there will inevitably come away throbbing with eagerness to share what has been seen *and felt* in some illuminating account. Nothing speaks more clearly and engagingly than a folk-level story—and the Bible is filled with them. No preaching succeeds so well as that which treats some biblical story and is true to a story-line in its substance and form. When preaching honors the principle of start, buildup, and resolution, especially as these relate to some person's experience of conflict or stress, it ensures immediacy, generates insight, and provides a means of hope, faith, change, and growth. Nothing stirs the chemistry of the consciousness and prods the self to commitment like good story preaching.

STORY AS A PRIMARY MODE IN SCRIPTURE

The Bible highlights storytelling as a major mode and medium. Gerhard von Rad has called attention in his writings to the way Israel used her historical and prophetic traditions to give fresh meanings to her people in new settings and circumstances, reciting and "retelling" [*Nacherzahlen*] her life with God so as

to influence the faith and behavior of the people. [1] Telling
and retelling the story about God's dealings with the nation was
done again and again for changing audiences and under ever-
changing skies, but always with concern to inform, confess,
remind, celebrate, witness, and be renewed.

Historical narratives abound in the Bible. [2] The reasons for
this are not far to seek. Narratives and stories deal with life and
living from a presentational level; they show life in concrete-
ness. What is elemental and enduring is portrayed best in
stories, stories that need not always give us exact history so long
as they are history-like. [3] The stories grant us depth-learning
because they engage us at the gut level of feeling as well as on the
mind level of realization. Reality and revelation conjoin in the
biblical narratives, and from them we gain a certain
understanding of God and a crucial understanding of ourselves.

The biblical narratives combine to show us a confessional
story regarding God's saving deeds. The Old Testament gives us
a basic unit-story from Abraham down to the times of the early
prophets, while the rest of the books from that early period
repeat and review elements from within that period. The story
calls attention to the determinative acts of God toward the
nation's fathers in Israel's pre-history, moves on to tell about
Israel's election by God in the Exodus, and then highlights the
covenant he established with them as his people. [4] But the story
widens in the New Testament to include the church, the "new
Israel" redeemed by the saving life and death of Jesus Christ and
sent on mission in the world. This part of the longer story is the
context of our own personal story as redeemed persons. The
whole Bible is confessional, and it provides an unlimited
province within which to search, study, and find, and from
which to teach and preach.

It is not by chance that stories are the major medium in giving
the biblical message. And since this is so, it follows that
preaching from the stories—and in story-fashion—is basically at

one with the materials themselves. There is a great power in preaching when we design sermons with concern for atmosphere, character, plot, tone, and movement, intent to serve the kerygma and the religious needs of those who hear us. [5]

STORY-PREACHING IN THE BLACK CHURCH TRADITION

In writing about the impact and eventfulness of story-preaching, I am recalling how apt that method has been in helping to shape many of my own biblical, doctrinal, and ethical perspectives. Growing up under able black preachers, I heard them gladly because of their contagion in "telling 'The Story'." This expression, "telling The Story," gathers up all that is related to the major theme of the Bible, but it focuses with special care upon the life and ministry of Jesus. In our way of speaking, "The Story" immediately recalls the history of his saving deed, the will of God at work in his life, and the effects of that deed when it is accepted in true faith.

James H. Cone has also called attention to story-preaching as a persuasive influence upon his life as a boy and his thought as a theologian. Cone tells us:

> In black churches, the one who preaches the Word is primarily a storyteller. And thus when the black church community invites a minister as pastor, their chief question is: "Can the Reverend tell the story?" This question refers to the theme of black religion and also to the act of storytelling itself . . . , creating a black vision of the future. [6]

Story-telling is not elementary but elemental: elemental for affirmation, argument, witness, meaning, impact, engagement, ethos, and emotion as well.

The power of recited story is unequaled. William Holmes Borders recalls the effects of that power upon him as he, eight years old at the time, sat in the morning service at Swift Creek

Baptist Church in rural territory just outside Macon, Georgia, spellbound as his pastor-father, James Buchanan Borders, preached and "told The Story." Sensing his call from God at that early age, young Borders accepted it and started on the long road he has followed as an honored preacher of the Gospel, "the Lord's handyman."[7] Open to "The Story" as it came to his ears, Borders found his heart gripped by its persuasive charm and claims.

So did James Herman Robinson when he was still a boy, deeply impressed by how Jim Haywood, his Baptist pastor, held forth at Knoxville's Mount Zion Baptist Church. Robinson confessed:

> I was stuck on the preacher, Jim Haywood, who was a magnificent actor, a challenging speaker, and a "Jim Dandy" dresser. . . . He was a natural-born storyteller and orator, full of spiritual fervor, hell and damnation language, and picturesque images. . . . He captivated me completely. I was oblivious to all else, the choir, the crowd, my aunt [with whom he sat]. When he finished I wanted to go right out and do something—any-thing—right then and there. I found myself thinking his thoughts.[8]

Story had stirred the chemistry of his consciousness; it had spoken to his whole self.

THE PRESENT TENSE IN STORY-LIFE

1. *Carefully designed story-preaching can give contemporary appeal to the biblical tradition.*

A large space of time and experience stands plotted and exposed in the biblical tradition. Since the whole of the Bible forms a large-scale retelling of the sacred story, the records report divine truth directed to use in the present tense. The patterned events recounted in the sacred pages are to be understood not as mere "ancient story," but as part of the graph of destiny, revealing pointers, clear transcripts of living experience; some distinctly historical, and others history-like, are preserved and related on purpose.[9] They offer a perspective that reveals; they present information that inspires faith and elicits a response.

I referred a few pages back to the engaging impact of story-preaching in the black church tradition. I also cited the personal statements of three well-known black leaders who recalled the way storytelling captured their attention and spoke so clearly to them in their childhood, both engaging and educating at one and the same time. There is more to this than meets the eye on a first look. Given the factors of controlled detail and timing, the preacher in each case had touched the listening youth at just that level of appeal. Young Cone, Borders, and Robinson were not reacting to the storytelling as a mere hypnotoform phenomenon. While it is quite possible that a dramatic telling of a story can appear as a hypnotic-style for some young minds and eyes, there is surely more to the effects of a story than the human touch of a skilled dramatist. There are understood states of mind because of the telling itself, levels of appropriation that match levels of appeal: a child will get caught up in the action in the story—seeing it; an adolescent will identify with the heroes, and perhaps the meaning the story holds; while an adult will catch the meaning and sift the ideas that lead to that meaning. Every hearer relates to any story, biblical or otherwise, in keeping with his or her experiences and needs and perception. Interestingly, no one contact with any biblical story is ever final in its impact upon us because the same story will speak to us on different levels at different times in our life; its appeal always contemporary with where we are. This can be made to happen when a narrative-story is used in a careful design.

2. A *carefully designed story-sermon can guide the imaging our hearers do.*

Preaching at its best will provide substance for imaging.

Imaging is common to humans, and we need it because it is the way we widen the parameters of our experience and envision new possibilities for ourselves. Imaging is our way of dreaming, our window on the world that stands just beyond where we now live. Jesus used stories as a regular method for preaching. So strong was his preference for storytelling, Mark tells us, that "he did not speak to them without a parable" (4:34a). Jesus so guided the imaging of his hearers that his critics were maddened by his control, while "the common people heard him gladly" (Mark 12:37 KJV).

Most humans like to be guided in imaging, in seeing what holds some promise for their lives, or what can give light at some heavy, dark, propositional point of concern. We all like the speaker who knows how and when to use an apt illustration to clarify and clinch some point while speaking. The illustration becomes the key that unlocks the door for many hearers, the window through which needed light falls to aid sight and grant insight. W. M. Taylor, in his Lyman Beecher Lectures at Yale many years ago, mentioned the art of Dr. Andrew Thomson (1779–1831) in this regard. Thomson would sometimes preach for at least two hours, we are told, and yet without losing his audience. Someone once asked Thomson what was the secret of holding his hearers over such a long stretch of time, and the preacher answered: "Whenever I see them get dull I throw in a story. I consider a story has an effect for twenty minutes."[10] Some stories have an effect for a lifetime. The biblical stories are of such character and forcefulness. They are worthy guides for the imaging we need to do about our lives.

The alert student of Scripture will be challenged by the persistent wisdom seen therein as the writers usually blend propositional statement and pictorial language. Again and again some doctrine is given by means of a picture, some truth stated by means of a story, some affirmation made, then given a visionary impact by means of narration.

The statement in Genesis 1:1 about the beginning of creation is one such instance, illustrating how propositional statement and pictorial language are wedded with visionary effect. The well-known verse reads, "In the beginning God created the heavens and the earth"; then follows the lengthy pictorial section about the process of creation. The propositional teaching is thus sharpened by the vision made possible through guided imaging.[11] The fact is that a way of thinking leads to a certain way of seeing and acting. Stories are powerful idea agencies; they bring matters and meanings quite vividly before the mind's eye.

Worthy preaching will honor the human capacity to imagine, and it will seek to direct that imaging with integrity. To this end, story-sermons are a practical modality for our task.

3. A *carefully planned story-sermon helps hearers to identify with the meanings about which stories speak.*

A story can harness a hearer to some truth. When that truth has insinuated itself into the hearer's consciousness, made its "shock" at a place of intense awareness, and has gripped the imagination in lively fashion, the hearer *feels* prodded and pulled. The character of the truth makes its claim. The hearer sees his or her personal history and opportunity in the light of an earlier history. The one plot unearths another; one episode "judges" another; one life yields a lesson to another person. The story meaning "locates" the hearer because it prods a near-instant identification.

The biblical stories continue to point beyond themselves, and through them believers can rehearse meanings by which faith is sustained. The stories represent those meanings so that the believer can appropriate them in new situations and be renewed. That is what happens when the story has a fixed, confessional base and meaning.

Rabban Gamaliel II, grandson of that famed leader cited in Acts (5:34; 22:3), was so impressed by the recital of the Exodus story that he urged: "In every generation a man must so regard himself as if he came forth himself out of Egypt, for it is written, *And thou shalt tell thy son in that day saying, when I came forth out of Egypt* [Ex. 13:8]. Therefore are we bound . . . to bless him who wrought all these wonders for our fathers and for us."[12]

The vitality of the story tradition shows itself again and again in the preaching of the cross. Katherine Hankey's "I Love to Tell the Story" is more than a song of sentiment; it is a reflection of the power of story that is still important in understanding and even actualizing the faith. Story helps us bridge the gap of history and participate in the meaning of an original, confessional, determinative event.

The case of narrative or story preaching need not be labored further. Such preaching releases to the hearer the testimonial power of scripture, creating impact and insight for the hearer's life and needs. Narrative is the biblical way of speaking. Each story carries more than a message and moral; it partakes of that genuine "spokenness" [*Gesprochenheit*], to use Martin Buber's choice word.[13]

"STORY" IN THE PREACHING OF JESUS

In any discussion of Jesus' preaching, we are face to face with preaching at its best. Jesus was alert to communicative design and he wedded substance and style, form and focus. The language and style embedded in the gospel tradition do indeed reveal the characteristics of his very voice (*ipsissima vox*). This is especially evident in the parabolic teaching and preaching attributed to him.[14]

The parables of Jesus are themselves sermons. Each one brings an insight to bear upon the hearer's consciousness by means of a living scene narrated. The hearer's attention is raised through dramatic confrontation with a sensed truth about God's relation to the human condition. True to sermon focus, each parable conveys a single message and demands a single response, and the parable's artful design gives the occasion of hearing unmistakable depth. The procedure in the parable is linked with the power of the story. Reality comes to focus in the telling, just as it must come to focus in any story sermon. The parable is actually a form of implied argument through its pictured life and plot; yet it does its work—and wins—because of the artful design to engage one and extract a feeling and response to the basic message.

The parables of Jesus show great variety on his part as a preacher. Some tell of God's gracious action (as in the parable of the lost sheep, the waiting father); some tell of God's unrelenting demand (as in the parable of the good Samaritan, the talents); and still others blend the prophetic, kerygmatic, pastoral, and didactic elements. The affective levels in narrative are great indeed.

It is instructive to observe the way Jesus sought to involve his hearers right from the start. Consider Luke's setting for the good Samaritan story (Luke 10:29-30), which he reports Jesus told in answer to a question put to him. Interestingly, the parable as we have it does not give a categorical answer to the one who questioned him, but the answer is within the province of the story itself, clearly sensed in the characteristic spirit and actions of the pictured "neighbor." The neighbor is not defined by Jesus, but by the audience *after* the story had disclosed its point. Stories are helpful as answering devices. They stir us at the suggestion level and pull upon our spirits in still more concrete fashion. Interestingly, Jesus did not leave that story at the suggestion level, but in a pastoral and prophetic spirit issued a call to all who heard it to fulfill its claim. Appealing to the self-consciousness of all his audience, Jesus directly addressed them with the word, "Go and do likewise" (Luke 10:3*b*).

READYING THE NARRATIVE SERMON

1. *Choose a narrative or story with a basic thrust to help the hearer understand and rightly handle the realities of life.* A story

is important because of its meaning and import, not because of its drama.

The testimonial and teaching power of biblical narratives are supremely relevant to this end. These stories blend biography, autobiography, sociology, and theology, allowing us to rehearse the faith, fate, or fortunes of other people. They let us see how decisions were made for good or ill, how someone acted in wisdom or folly, what was gained or lost because of the deed, and God's assessment. The biblical stories show us praiseworthy souls and fools. The stories let us see the way God ridiculed futile attempts of men to conceal their sins, as in the case of Achan and David, giving perspective on the need to "come clean" in confession and repentance. We learn through the stories that pride and high-handedness are always defeated in the end, that the arrogant use of power—as in the hands of Pharaoh and Nebuchadnezzar—is doomed right from the start. The stories in scripture let us lament with those who fail—like Esau, David, and Peter; wait with persons tested by time and circumstances whose view is on the future—like Abraham and Sarah, Moses, and Hannah.

The stories can help us learn from those who doubted, like Thomas; those who drifted, like Jacob and Demas; those who chose the low way, like Judas. The stories pull back the curtain and show us the intimate dealings of God with honest souls: Isaiah, renewed after that temple theophany; Samson, blind, shackled, but penitent after his sortie into unheeding lust; Peter, surprised by forgiveness as he is recommissioned by the risen Lord after a headlong plunge into a world of lies to save his skin; Saul of Tarsus, a chosen vessel after that Damascus Road encounter with the Lord of the church. Hearers can locate themselves in the light of strategic stories and the points of reference they provide. The stories can be used to help the hearer escape the routine, go beyond what is inept, tighten what is loose, see what cannot be fully explained, and gain what need never be lost. The biblical narratives are supremely important to the preacher in any attempt to help hearers feel what Ralph Waldo Emerson once referred to as the "sharp peaks and edges of truth."

2. *Immerse yourself in the story until its basic issue is understood and its living thrust is felt.* The story must become a word-event for the preacher before it can live in the retelling.

The story must be felt at the animated level of its reported happening. There is action taking place in the story, and that action has a reason. Persons are involved in acting and responding, and there is an issue in it all. The stories offer us no titles, so one must study the narratives with care until the true focus is understood and the import makes its suggestive impact.

The need to immerse oneself deeply in a narrative to gain its truth can be fulfilled only by a firsthand and unhurried mastery of the biblical account. Late planning leads one into temptation—the temptation to gather someone else's work, and in quick fashion, using it all without depth of treatment and personal involvement. Any preacher takes a big risk in preaching what has been gathered or thought about in haste. Late planning can lead to gross errors in detail, stress, and thoughtful application of the insight in a passage. Narrative preaching demands a firsthand acquaintance with the materials and what those materials mean.

Miss Marian Anderson tells of a time in her early girlhood school days when she overheard the singing class through the wall of the adjoining room in which she and her classmates were studying. Stirred by her love for music, young Marian lost track of what her own teacher up in the front of the room was saying. The day came when it was her turn to go to singing class next door, and when the music started young Marian lit into the melody with great gusto and full volume of voice. Having listened through the wall to the other singing class across the days, she felt confident about the music.

But the music teacher soon approached her, tapped her on the shoulder and asked, "Marian, what are you singing?" Marian proudly answered, "Sleep, Polly, sleep"! The teacher chided her for not looking at the words on the page before her. Marian looked—and the words she should have been singing were "Peacefully sleep"! She had been singing at secondhand, echoing what had come muffled through the wall.[15]

Preaching without firsthand acquaintance with a text or narrative can also lead to embarrassment. Repeating some traditional account, and embellishing it with fervor and at full voice, only to discover later that many details did not ring true to the original account, can cause deep embarrassment and chagrin, not to mention the sad fact that as a trumpet, the sermon gave "an uncertain sound" (I Cor. 14:8 KJV).

Preaching on scriptural narratives calls for close and careful study. The preacher must be fully acquainted with the story and be prepared to deal with its seven components: the characters, action, setting, form, language, style, and meaning.[16] Only in this way can a proper overview and inside-feel essential for shaping a narrative sermon occur.

3. *Locate the vertical point of divine action on the horizontal line of the story. The functional import of the narrative usually emerges there.* It is with that import that the relevant narrative sermon should seek to deal.

Once the import of the narrative has been sensed, then the functional use of it in a sermon can begin. But not in a simple recounting of the story verbatim. The story is to be preached, not just repeated.

Walter C. Kaiser, Jr., has recently suggested:

Nothing can be more discouraging and disheartening for contemporary believers gathered to hear the Word of God than to listen to the simple recounting and bare description of an Old Testament or Gospel narrative as an excuse for expository preaching. This kind of preaching is nothing more than narrating a "B.C. story" or "first century A.D. homily" which merely engages in stringing verses or events together, rather than attempting to come to terms with the truth taught by the writer in that narrative.[17]

That is the concern of narrative preaching: to come to terms with the truth carried by the narrative. Kaiser suggests that this is best done by "principalizing a biblical passage," by which he means discovering the "enduring ethical, spiritual, doctrinal, and moral truths or principles which the writer himself set forth by the way in which he selected his details and arranged the contextual setting of his narrative." This process is the same as that of locating the point of intersection between the human story and God's signal relation to the action in it. When this is done, the preacher has bridged the distance between the original setting of the story and the present situation of those who will hear the sermon.

4. *Stay in the background as the storyteller: maintain sufficient detachment to let the storyline make its point, lest your own point of view dull the intended impact of the narrative.*

Enhance interest in the storyline by beginning at a point where the action can be interrupted without loss of focus. The sermon "The Rock That Moved," by Peter Marshall, is an excellent illustration of this kind of beginning, and from an understood "detached reporter" stance.[18] But there is more than report; there is appeal and a distinct call within the treatment. As the sermon ends, the hearing person has heard a word of hope and possibility for change: "Christ changed Simon into Peter, the sinner into the saint. He can change your life, if you are willing!" Marshall moved the hearer from being a spectator into the stance of someone who also needs the understanding, changing touch of Christ. The main thrust of his message was carried in his storyline and deepened by a calculated distance as the storyteller. Peter Marshall excelled as a narrative preacher.[19] Although detached, he made the *story-experience* live.

5. *Watch the narrator's way of working, and take cues for your sermon approach and design from his treatment.*

The conditions in the story are important to the sermon line. The consequences from the action must be given their due regard. Billy Graham's sermon "The Prodigal Son" follows the logical sequences of the parable Jesus gave and makes the same point of highlighting the receptive love of a longing Father-God for his erring, lost children.[20]

(My story sermon in chapter 7, "Anatomy of a Failure," took its cues from the narrator's adversative use of "but". See II Sam. 11:1, 9, 13, 27—the pivotal text—and 12:12.)

6. *Experiment with many narrative styles until you discover and shape your most fruitful approach for handling a story-sermon.*

There are many such styles: preaching in the first-person role, sermonizing a short story, delivering a letter sermon, or doing a modern parable. An illuminating example of first-person preaching is seen in David O. Woodyard's "A Certain Dumb Man," an I-narrative form based on Luke 11:14-28, the account of an exorcism.[21] The best examples of the short-story sermon approach are found in Robert E. Luccock's *Lost Gospel: And Other Sermons Based on Short Stories.*[22] Martin Luther King, Jr., left a powerful witness and a model letter sermon form in his "Paul's Letter to American Christians," one of the seventeen sermons in his book *Strength to Love.*[23] Additional examples of the story style are seen in the work of Frank W. Boreham (1871–1959), who was one of the world's most honored and respected masters of narrative preaching.[24]

A STUBBORN FACT AND FAITH

We live our days under the impact of stories, some factual, some fictional, and others "factional," to use Alex Haley's new description of fictional fact. A day would not be normal without some story coming to our attention, even if it only takes shape as fancy in our own imagination.[25] The stories we hear about contemporary happenings and the interpretations offered about their expected effects, all tone our working days and challenge our waking hours. There are the presentiments of television, the blared news-notes of the radio, and the bold headlines of the daily press; and the concern is always the same: to give us the stories.

Our Christian faith presents The Story. That faith is a confessional report about the determinative deed of God in Christ to come and save us from our sins and relate us fully to himself as our Father and God. Preaching serves the interests of that faith.

Many years ago Phillips Brooks (1835–1893) called attention to the importance of this story as he addressed seminarians and preachers gathered to hear the Lyman Beecher Lectures at Yale. Brooks declared, "I am sure that the more fully you come to count your preaching the telling of a message, the more valuable and real the church will become to you, the more true will seem to you your brotherhood with all messengers of that same message in all strange dresses and in all strange tongues."[26]

III. DESIGNING THE
TEXTUAL/EXPOSITORY SERMON

A word is in order about the chapter title, which implies a relation between textual and expository preaching. That word is in order because homiletical theorists have long distinguished between those sermon types, classifying them on the basis of the amount of scripture used as foundational message. The chapter title above suggests that the distinction is an arbitrary one and should be disregarded when exploration of the biblical message is the essential concern. Dwight E. Stevenson has put it well: "The distinction between textual and expository preaching, based on length alone, is artificial and should be abandoned. All biblical preaching is at one and the same time textual and expository; it is based upon a text which it expounds."[1]

Exposition is both a method and a result, a process and a production. The result or production is occupied mainly with showing the message and import of a unit of scripture, while the process followed in doing so is that of "mining" the unit and explaining it in order to bring out to the hearers what is there for them. Rightly understood and done, the point of it all is not to explain a scripture unit merely, thus increasing the hearer's knowledge of the Bible, but to afford the hearers guidance and insight for change, growth, and a responsible life of faith.

The expository sermon should be focused, interesting, and

life-oriented. Henry Sloane Coffin (1877–1954), in his Warrack lectures of 1926, told the Scottish seminarians and divines he was addressing to give increased attention to expository preaching, not just to teach the Bible "but to interpret life by the Bible."[2] In this way, the ancient but timely Word escapes the cold confinement of print, loses its "back-thereness," and becomes an encountering voice in the hearer's life. Expository sermons, rightly planned and rightly oriented, should always have this as their reason, while using scripture as their resource.

Would-be expositors will find themselves in a noble and select tradition of workers. The historical study of the expository method will introduce one to an ancient concern and a wide range of leaders and methods. There are insights to be gained from those who preached to the church in the apostolic period, as Richard N. Longenecker has shown, calling attention to their Christocentric perspective on using their Bible (Old Testament).[3] The homilies and commentaries of the Church Fathers are grand proof of their concern and expository toil, and how they made their preaching apply to problems and needs then current.

Origen (184–254) has been credited with the expositional method most widely used today. Athanasius (297–373) and Bishop Augustine (354–430) were both informed in his method of sermonizing, but Augustine's background and skills in rhetoric made his the more stylish mode. Book Four of Augustine's classic work *On Christian Doctrine* treats preaching style, offering that able expositor's methods for handling biblical substance, which he discussed in Books One, Two, and Three.[4] Augustine's way of wedding words and scripture teachings was exemplary, an evident mark of his interest and industry as well as "genius."

The tradition is found in a long line of worthy preachers. The standard histories treat them, but Yngve Brilioth's (1891–1964) brief but jam-packed *Brief History of Preaching* also outlines the connection of these preachers with one another through that

preaching method.[5] After surveying Brilioth's historical treatment of the expositors, one would be well advised to turn
directly to their sermons. That study should finally extend, of
course, to recent and contemporary masters of the expository
method. A list of them should include Charles Reynolds Brown
(1862–1950), G. Campbell Morgan (1863–1945), F. B. Meyer
(1847–1929), Donald Grey Barnhouse (1895–1960), Sandy F.
Ray (1898–1979), George Arthur Buttrick (1892–1980), Paul S.
Rees, Harold John Ockenga, James S. Stewart, Samuel G.
Hines, and James M. Boice, among others.

SOME GUIDELINES AND EXAMPLES

1. *Study your given text or passage at firsthand until its
setting, form, and insight are clear to you.*

There are passages that you can probe on your own and quite
readily understand them, and there are other passages that will
demand the help of professional exegetes and commentators to
make your study fruitful. Think and pray your way into the
passage, going as far as you can go without others helping you;
then, as you see the barriers posed by questions you cannot
answer, seek the help of the experts. However long this process
of personal investigation must take, the time spent is always
worth it when the purpose is to bless someone's life through
what you find.

Behind every text is its setting. Within every text is a form.
The purpose of the text is insight or message. That message must
be understood before it can be abstracted for use in a sermon. A
text is "abstracted" when a truth or theme is drawn from it.[6] The
sermon must develop out of the preacher's thought about some
feature or features seen in the text, and this selective interest
always makes the sermon a narrower product than the text itself
is. The text is given; the sermon is created. The sermons we
create are always less than the texts we use. This is what separates

our *words* from his *Word,* but it is also what helps that Word to speak its voice in ever-new accents to oncoming, ongoing generations. It is this that constitutes the great mystery of preaching.

The fuller message of the text breaks through increasingly when the sermon matches its mood and spirit as well as serves its meaning. This is one reason that many expositors insist on keeping even their rhetoric allied with the textual wording. Their concern is to be commended, but a preacher does have the freedom to take the "message-germ" and work it in a fresh way, applying its insight in words and ways the intended hearers will readily perceive. A good expository sermon is not a quotation of the text or passage; it is an exposition of its meaning and import.

A close, firsthand study of any text will make its demands upon us, but the rewards are greater. That higher word grants a message that makes a difference, first in the preacher, then in those who hear what the preacher reports.

Expository sermons are not the mere result of ingenuity in manipulating a text. Good exposition demands being mastered by that text. The "exposition" should rightly be about what the text(ual passage) has *spoken* to the preacher. And the biblical texts *do* speak. The text is language in use, a formally structured statement by which some author has sought to declare, discuss, or depict something having to do with man's life in the light of God. As the preacher "listens" to what is being spoken, the realization deepens that scripture is not a set of mere document-texts but a collection of voice-texts: thus the rightful definition of scripture as "Word of God."[7]

The text was given to preserve its message beyond the moment—in this sense it is a document; but that text was sometimes sent to carry its message beyond the place of writing, as a stand-in for the messenger in his absence. The writer is always a potent presence in any message, which is why I prefer to speak of scripture as voice-texts. A hearing relationship develops as the preacher studies a biblical passage, and after having been heard, the message is clear for a fresh announcement and application through preaching.

The immediate goal of the firsthand study of any text, then, is to hear its message. The message is the basis for the exposition.

2. *Whenever possible, let the textual passage determine your outline and tone of treatment.*

This means wrestling with the biblical writer's structured statement, and watching for how he wedded function with form.

Scripture study involves us in observing some formal ways of writing. The basic forms we encounter there are story, statements, expressions, and prescriptives. Some attention has been given in an earlier chapter on "story," so it is not necessary to deal with that category again at this point. But the other three descriptive categories must receive fuller mention now.[8]

a) *Statements*. These are the sentences biblical writers straightforwardly used in reporting or affirming certain facts.

Genesis 1:1—"In the beginning God created the heavens and the earth."

Acts 12:1—"About that time Herod the king laid violent hands upon some who belonged to the church."

b) *Expressions*. These are forms of writing in which emotion and impulse are purposely active, and for cause.

Romans 11:33—"O the depth of the riches and wisdom and knowledge of God: How unsearchable are his judgments and how inscrutable his ways!"

John 20:28—"Thomas answered him, 'My Lord and my God!' "

c) *Prescriptives*. These are directions about something to be done.

Romans 12:13—"Contribute to the needs of the saints, practice hospitality."

Ephesians 5:11—"Take no part in the unfruitful works of darkness, but instead expose them."

The language in Scripture is dynamic. It reports facts to be understood and believed. Statements are used to announce, assert, and affirm those facts. Biblical language is filled with expressions, because feelings erupted as the Christian work was progressing, and as new experiences deepened believers in the faith. Prescriptives also abound in scripture, because the writers knew that grace demands an imperative along with an indicative.[9] Truth emerges in all of the stated forms, but the tone of treating that truth in a sermon is often suggested by the formal tone of the writer's words.

This means that the would-be expositor must live with the passage long enough to learn its message, on the one hand, and discern its patterned outlay and tone, on the other. As Morgan Phelps Noyes once wrote: "The truth is that the preacher must come at his message by a double process. He must *work* laboriously for it, using all the resources of the spiritual and intellectual life in his search for truth. At the same time, he must *receive* it."[10] That is always the case with an expositor, and that receiving happens when the text is confronted in the spirit of a listener.

3. *Summarize the textual message into a paragraph, then let your preaching concerns dictate how much of its insight(s) to use now, or later.*

If the passage was short and its structure simple, one sermon might carry the weight of the message it speaks. There is an implied principle here: the longer the passage, the more sermons one might need to plan to carry the cargo of its intended contribution. This doubtless explains the long-hallowed homiletical custom of insisting that a sermon should be based upon one text and that the text should be short, "a small enough packet to be carried easily in the memory."[11]

But much depends upon the expositor's methods, skill in

designing, and the purpose that dictates how some scripture portion is to be used. Dwight E. Stevenson has long advocated preaching on whole biblical books, sometimes as an overview in beginning a series of sermons on the contents of some respective book, but also because "the biblical books themselves [are] the most natural units of scripture imaginable—and the most neglected in the shaping of sermons."[12] But if one is not that ambitious, there are the dialogues of Scripture, the parables, treasured psalms, all of which allow for singular treatment of natural units.

4. *Sermonize the message, with your eye always upon how it is to apply to human interest and experience.*

There are four basic ways in which sermonic exposition can go askew. One is the slavish restatement of the textual setting at times when it can be assumed, or touched upon lightly. A second is belaboring what is obvious, doing exhaustively what should be done suggestively and with stress upon application. A third way exposition fails is when the preacher uses the same pattern of progression to deal with very different textual genres. The fourth problem to be faced in designing an expository sermon is in assuming that attention to the text(ual passage) is enough by itself to produce an adequate sermon.

There *are* those times when a textual setting can be assumed, allowing time for the preacher to do something *with* it rather than spend unnecessary time *on* it. Billy Graham did that in his sermon "The Prodigal Son." Graham began: "Now tonight, let's turn to the 15th chapter of Luke. I'm not going to read the passage because it's too long, but it is a familiar story that all of us have read and heard since childhood. It's called "The Story of the Prodigal Son.""[13]

Then Graham went on to deepen the impression of the story upon the hearers' minds, suggesting that there were more levels to it than the one most familiar to people. After referring to it in the previous sentence as the story of the prodigal son, he teachingly commented: "That's what we call it. There are many ways we could term this passage from Luke's Gospel. It could be called 'The Story of the Loving Father.' It could be called 'The Story of the Church Member Without Christ,' because that is exactly what the elder brother was."

The rest of the sermon is an expositional account of facts of the parable, with intermittent application and evangelistic appeal. Despite his free-speech style, Graham did not belabor the obvious, but spent the time pressing home the message on several levels at once.

No one sermon design will fit every textual genre with similar success. Every textual style demands and deserves its own mode of treatment in keeping with its mood. It is necessary to say this, the much-honored works of Alexander Maclaren (1826–1910) and Frederick William Robertson (1816–1853) notwithstanding. Robertson's two-point contrast method in treating a text or passage was used for most of his sermonic work. The principle of balancing aspects of a text was not original with him, but Robertson lifted it to new heights. Influenced by Rector Archibald Boyd, with whom he served at Christchurch in Cheltenham, England, for a time, Robertson "adapted this method, developed it, made it characteristically his own, and by his example finally spread it to the ends of the English-speaking world," biographer James R. Blackwood explains.[14] While the conciseness of this design allowed one to deal with the message substance, and in fuller measure, there was the problem of always having to find contrasts in every text or passage chosen. Robertson did, but that is a tribute to his sermonic greatness and not to any absoluteness in his characteristic sermon method.[15]

Alexander Maclaren was justly famous for his pulpit work, but he used three points for nearly every sermon, a structure he confessed as a natural reaction in his mind as he studied a text. Writer W. Robertson Nicoll, in an obituary tribute to Maclaren as published in *The British Weekly* when he died in 1910, commented:

> Every one knows his method of preaching. His people, as one of his friends said, "were fed with the three-pronged fork." He had an extraordinary gift of analyzing a text. He touched it . . . and it immediately broke up into [three] natural and memorable divisions, so comprehensive and so clear that it seemed wonderful that the text should have been handled in any other way.[16]

But most texts can be handled in more than one way. The would-be expositor must necessarily experiment now and again to find the best expression for a message. But the form and focus of the message in the text will make certain urges on their own as the alert preacher listens to the text and works with it.

I did that in preparing an expository series on the Epistle to the Hebrews for radio use. Fifteen sermons were shaped after long study of the Epistle, and all fell under the general theme "Jesus and Our Human Pilgrimage." One of the sermons, "He Was Faithful," appears in chapter 7 of this book.

Intending to make substantial use of the Epistle itself, I pursued the following process in shaping the design of that sermon.

  I. The Hermeneutical Procedure
     Section treated: Hebrews 3:1-6
     a) Jesus exalted as supreme example of fidelity to trust.
        The passage is an artful blend of history, theology, and doctrine. The passage interests, instructs, inspires. The writing is closely knit, with two persons contrasted but honored—Moses and Jesus. The reason is given in the text. The issue at hand among the readers was the need for strength to stand up under pressure of persecution, as did Jesus.

b)   The passage lends itself to a pastoral purpose: encouragement of persons under great stress and strain because of their faith.

3:1 A conclusive beginning—a call made to "consider [*katanoēsate*, aorist imperative, fix the mind upon in order to discern and decide] Jesus." The reason for doing so follows. The titles applied to Jesus increase the weightedness of his example before them.

3:2 "Faithful being" [Gr. *pistos onta*]. Piety is indicated, an attitude of worshipful belonging, total obedience, allegiance. Jesus was fully inclined toward God as the one who appointed him. The present tense of the participle suggests a characteristic stance of Jesus toward God.

"Just as Moses." A comparison is in view, arguing from the lesser to the higher, but with clear indications of their correspondence:

i) both Moses and Jesus were deliverers,
ii) both were intercessors,
iii) both were prophets,
iv) both had "face-to-face" dealing with God,
v) Moses gave the law; Jesus, the gospel,
vi) both were suffering servants,
vii) both established covenants,
viii) both had titles by God's appointment.

3:3 "much more glory than Moses."

II. The Homiletical Procedure[17]

Title: taken from text (3:2), "He Was Faithful"

a) represents a summary of the section message
b) offers a propositional and pictorial image
c) allows a biographical treatment for the message

What appears above was taken directly from notes made as the text was being "interrogated" and "mined" for its message, tone, flow of argument, and possible application to experience. The full result of the sermonic process is seen in the sermon itself.

THE LURE OF THE IDEAL

Expository sermons can be done, and should be done. They reflect the best offered in the texts, and it is the text that brings the message. Preaching wedded to a text brings forth spiritual fruit, while talk without a text becomes a pretext that deserves to be questioned.

Paul Hindemith, contemporary musician-composer who was always going forward in his music, both in form and in content, commented that however far he ranged on his harmonic journeys as a musician, he would always have to come back at the end of a piece to a simple tonic chord. It was his conviction that the listener needed not only flights into other worlds of sound than the normal constructions allowed, but also a return to firm and native ground. Thus these two sentences from one of his writings: "Music, as long as it exists, will always take its departure from the major triad and return to it. The musician cannot escape it any more than the painter his primary colours or the architect his three dimensions."[18]

True preaching takes its departure from the word of God, in the sermon, but must forever return to that Word. Expository preaching, carefully planned and rightly done, keeps preacher and people at home *with* and *in* the biblical message, always close to the heart of the matter—the great salvation events of which the Bible is record, reminder, and forecast.

IV. DESIGNING THE
DOCTRINAL/TOPICAL SERMON

The church began under the contagious ministry of an itinerant teaching preacher. Those who heard him interpret the life of man in the light of God gladly called him rabbi. Jesus of Nazareth knew the serious service of doctrine and he gave himself fully to that service. On one occasion, being interrogated by Pilate, Jesus declared, "For this I was born, and for this I have come into the world, to bear witness to the truth" (John 18:37*b*). It was the teaching *by* him that gathered the first members of the church. It was teaching *about* him that helped that church deepen its roots and grow.

The church across the ages has always needed and expected a teaching ministry.[1] Henry Sloane Coffin reminded us that Jesus "was usually called Teacher," then added, "and it would be ·viser for Christian preachers to strive to be worthy of that title."[2] That is the point of concern in this chapter which explores the preacher's opportunity to teach and develop the people of God through preaching doctrine.

THE NEW TESTAMENT FOCUS ON DOCTRINE

The New Testament writings are filled with teaching. The materials reflect the apostolic stress upon "sound doctrine"and

its relation to right living.[3] The leaders in the early church took
seriously the need to deal with the awakened, questioning mind
and the questing soul; they dealt with that need by a careful
handling of truth. Their task was elemental. The Epistles show
that the writers took seriously where the believers were in their
thought and living, and that they preached and taught in vital
relation to that positioned level of need. First Timothy 3:2
categorically states that a pastor must be "an apt teacher,"
showing that a teaching role was expected because needed. It is
not necessary to join the debate over whether a clear distinction
should be drawn between preaching and teaching in the early
church; it is enough to say that the primary leaders followed the
lead Jesus took in pioneering the way before them—they
proclaimed as they taught, and they made their teachings
preach.[4]

Donald M. Baillie (1887–1954) told of addressing a group of
preachers on the subject of how to preach Christian doctrine.
While lecturing, Baillie confessed deep regret that his previous
pastoral ministry had not been devoted more heavily to
teaching, and he followed this up by saying that if he had to
begin again in a pastorate he would give himself more to being a
teacher for his people. (He was now a seminary professor.)
When he made the same admission to one of his divinity classes,
one of the students asked Baillie whether his present work had
not made him think that way. Baillie admitted the fairness of the
question, but then went on to assure the student that serious
thought had been given to the statement, and that he truly felt
the need for more emphasis by pastors on doctrine as they
preach.[5]

Those preachers who see their work as the sharing of an
all-important *message* will increasingly see the meaning of that
message in its truths, truths that do not change but into which
our interest and inquiry can more deeply extend their roots.
That is how Paul viewed his calling: "to preach to the Gentiles

the unsearchable riches of Christ, and to make all men see [*phōtisai*] what is the plan for the mystery hidden for ages in God who created all things" (Eph. 3:8*b*-9), and he fulfilled his task by sharing truths. Paul preached doctrine, with applied meaning. So did Peter, who was eager to remind those who knew his teachings to remain "established in the truth that you have" (II Pet. 1:12). The early church took doctrine seriously, and the New Testament reflects that fact in grand fashion.

DOCTRINE: FAITH'S GROUND PLAN

P. T. Forsyth (1848–1921) once wrote that preaching "is the Gospel prolonging and declaring itself."[6] Doctrinal preaching is that gospel explaining itself in the interest of a ground plan for the hearer's life and faith.

"Doctrine" has to do with the teaching of truths necessary for faith and salvation. Once taught those truths, the believer needs to understand their relation to life, and thus be able to apply them to personal and social experience.

The Old Testament words for doctrine carry the meaning of what is necessary to be known in order to fit God's norm: there is *leqach*, "what is received (as authoritative and binding);" there is *musar*, meaning "instruction"; and *shemuah*, "what has been heard (from someone with authority to teach and advise)." The New Testament writings build on that same set of understandings, but against a Greek background, with its main words of doctrine being: *didaskalia*, "something being taught (with a sense of purpose)"; *paradosis*, "something being handed down (passed on with a sense of its importance and authority)"; and *logos*, "an authoritative statement."[7]

Doctrinal preaching allows the preacher to fulfill his or her responsibility as a church teacher in mass fashion, as it were, passing on the truths of the faith in a community setting and in the spirit of worship. This is valuable for both preacher and congregation. It enables the church to receive truth, while it helps the preacher develop beyond the limits of being only an exhorter. W. E. Sangster wrote: "Some preachers are only exhorters. It is an honorable office, recognized in the New Testament. Yet happy is that congregation whose preacher is a teacher as well."[8]

The adequate preaching of doctrine is done only after great cost on the preacher's part. There is the cost in time and study and thought and prayer. Working over a period of time, a preacher can gain a fruitful understanding of some doctrine, and also insight into how it relates increasingly to life and faith. The sermon on a doctrine needs to be *biblically based* (exegetically sound and contextually honest), *authentically Christian* (at the New Testament level of biblical faith), and *experientially oriented* (related to the hearer's life and needs). These kinds of results *demand* prior thought, some consultation, and honest, fervent prayer. These results also demand working through one's own belief-system to expand and refine it—sometimes through the trauma of inward change—together with the willingness to confess that one has come to see and understand a truth as never before. As Richard John Neuhaus has commented, "A Christian congregation has a right to expect that their preacher and teacher has thought, read, pondered, puzzled, and prayed over the matter at hand and that he is prepared to share the harvest."[9] In doing so, however, the preacher might also have to pay the price at times when his or her convictional sharing meets misunderstanding, disagreement, and opposition in some hearers.

A.W.W. Dale, biographer of his famous preacher-father R. W. Dale (1829–1895), told of that preacher's experiences along this line. Quite early in his ministry Dale sensed the importance of systematic doctrinal instruction to the spiritual understanding and vigor of a church. Busy in the church from his youth, Dale early saw that "in many cases spiritual ardour is enfeebled and depressed through an imperfect apprehension of the primary truths of the gospel."[10] So he covenanted with God to be a doctrinal preacher, and he set about the business of guiding his hearers in "the discussion of the loftier problems of life and faith." And he paid the price in both success and suffering.

Forty or more years later, looking back on how it all began, R. W. Dale related to someone an experience from his first days of tempest and toil in the Birmingham, England, Carr's Lane Church. It happened that Dale met a certain honored preacher along one of Birmingham's streets, and they talked for awhile. The other preacher was older, and he talked with the younger Dale in a friendly way about his ministry. "I hear," he questioned, "that you are preaching doctrinal sermons to the congregation at Carr's Lane." Then he added, summarily, "They will not stand it." To which Dale replied, perhaps with some self-confidence, "They will have to stand it." The years between had shown that they could, that they would, and that they appreciated and grew through it. But not everyone. There were those among his hearers who wanted what they liked, and not what Dale thought they needed. His success in doctrinal preaching was a mingled one of personal stress in preparing and persevering in the face of dissenters.

Doctrinal preaching always costs, but it informs, convicts, inspires, and nurtures the individual believer and the church. When the preaching is planned with a view to their needs; when it is planned sufficiently well ahead to allow time for proper thought and structuring to result; when it has reasonable range as well as reason; and when it is backed by prayer so that it can both inform and inspire, doctrinal preaching becomes an indisputable spiritual resource for those who hear and receive it.

THE DOCTRINAL SERMON

1. In preparing to preach a doctrinal theme, *choose a teaching that is vital to human experience and hope*. The sermon can be

both prophetic and pastoral when its doctrinal core is seen alongside some experience, hope, or need.

The serious service of doctrine is to inform and inspire. Doctrine puts life in scriptural perspective. It provides that point of reference by which hearers can rightly interpret life, all of it. Neuhaus explains, "Such points of reference are doctrines, and the most essential of them are dogmas."[11] It is through sound doctrine that the preacher helps the hearer to see the variousness of life with clear eyes, an informed mind, and an understanding, responsible heart.

2. To buttress that teaching and provide scope for it, *use a strong text—or a reasonable combination of agreeable texts.* The concern is not to proof-text the doctrinal point, but to provide a scriptural center for the message. Under right handling, that scriptural center helps the light to shine out of the cluster of the preacher's structured words.

A topical concordance or index will be of help in locating relevant texts for chosen topics. Living with a text or two for awhile will finally convince one of its import and possibilities of use. Once the text or passage is chosen, the direct tie-in with the doctrinal theme or topic can be settled and the treatment designed.

3. As you interpret the text, *keep in mind the tradition of its use in the communion to which you belong, and depart from that tradition only when your firsthand study of scripture requires that you do so.*

Doctrinal preaching is best done as one "consults" with the history of the people who hear it. Denominational understandings and emphases must be given their due, and reinforced where necessary. Most church people have had some teaching given them. There is some formulation of the faith already at work in their minds. A preacher's predecessors in a certain pulpit doubtless laid basic teachings upon the foundation of their faith, and some larger framework of confession was followed in doing so. The historic denominations have their creeds and compendia of truths they hold as central, so the doctrinal preacher is not essentially alone as he or she works to prepare the teaching sermon for the people. That group history and understanding should be regarded as we do our work.

There are times, however, when one's firsthand study of scripture will lead to fresh accents regarding a given truth, or even to a reformulation of statement about an accepted church teaching.

Paul S. Rees told some years ago of a preacher-friend whose study of scripture led him to review his understanding about baptism.[12] The friend had been in contact with church groups beyond his own denominational context, serving them on occasion, and being challenged by the fruitful fellowship and spiritual interchange. His church background honored the tradition of infant baptism, but the day came when his study of scripture stirred him to believe that "believer's baptism" alone was a clear New Testament demand and that it should be allowed in his group. He shared his concern with the archbishop of the diocese, and asked if his new understanding should bar him from continued memberhip in that communion. The archbishop wisely advised him to remain with their church, and then approvingly confessed, "I wish for the day when our communion will recognize both modes of baptism."

All seemed to go along well after that, until that preacher's vicar was succeeded by a man who did not share such a broad view as the archbishop. And the new man let his difference of opinion be known. One day the vicar said to him, "Every time I give you the Holy Communion I feel sick to my stomach." Paul Rees explains, "All because he had learned that the man held Baptist views."

Doctrinal issues keep us reminded of our relation to the rest of the church. Our preaching of doctrine should honor that relation. The truth has been given, much of it well-formulated, and a history has been shaped through its use. Doctrinal preaching helps to pass the truth on, but along with it the history of interpretation to which one gives allegiance. When our insights into those teachings deepen or our perspectives change, any independent departures from the general group views should be publicized in sermons with great simplicity, sympathetic bearing, scriptural backing, and the awareness of risk.

In an expository-doctrinal series on Romans, R. W. Dale had to deal with 5:19, "For as by one man's disobedience many were made sinners, so by one man's obedience many will be made righteous." His treatment differed from the standard view of the Carr's Lane people about original sin and natural depravity. "Excitement deepened into alarm, and alarm rose to the height of a panic," Dale's biographer son reports. As the anxiety of the church members expanded to include misgivings from others beyond their circle, one old fellow-student—a man not given to much humor—said to Dale: "I wish that Paul had never written that chapter: it has greatly disturbed your position at Carr's Lane." But Paul had written that chapter, and Dale felt under necessity to think his way into it in order to preach its message with understanding. John Angell James, his older co-pastor there at the time, helped quiet much of the furor as he told those who disagreed with his younger colleague that the theological differences between them did not touch "the substance or core of Evangelical truth." James outrightly told some older, more hostile critics in the church to "leave the young man alone. He has the root of the matter in him," adding that Dale "must have his fling."

Dale did, and he learned much from it. He learned especially to center attention upon the central facts of the gospel and not the theories by which the facts are interpreted. He learned to distinguish forever between substance and expression in his quest to share the truths of the faith. Those who desire to preach doctrinal sermons must keep this ever in mind. They must guard against disruptive expressions as they seek to serve the truth, and refuse to preach doctrine for their own needs.

4. *Develop the doctrinal statement in thesis or question-and-answer form, and work progressively to build a climax of understanding to be harnessed for practical use.*

Donald M. Baillie's sermon "The Doctrine of the Trinity" is an excellent example of such a design.[13] In his first three sentences Baillie is off and running. Observe sentence number one: a reference to the church year setting of the service, and an announcement of his subject. "On this Trinity Sunday I wish to speak about the doctrine of the Trinity." Sentence number two is an admission that the subject is not a popular one, and is apt to be uninviting to many: "That sounds formidable and uninviting." A disarming word is sounded, but humanely and humbly. Then follows a statement of necessity to probe the subject: "But surely we ought not to shirk the task of understanding it." The introduction—short, terse, well-sequenced, soon ends with a motivational sentence that invites further inquiry: "And I believe we can find the whole Christian Gospel summed up in this mysterious doctrine, of three Persons, Father, Son and Holy Spirit, in one God." Then, a communal spirit is shown on the preacher's part, as he invitationally requests, "Let us try."

Baillie's outline shows three points, and they follow the flow of the text he used. "In the name of the Father, and of the Son, and of the Holy Ghost" (Matt. 28:19). But his treatment is not textual mainly; rather it is historical, because he unfolds the text against the background of the history by which it is to be understood. His argument is that God was first experienced, showing himself as singular and sovereign; that Jesus Christ was then experienced, showing God in a fresh way to men, making them sense that God was in him—as Father; and that the Holy Spirit was then experienced, overwhelming the disciples with a sense of the presence and power of God. The explanation culminates with a conclusive statement: "And that is how Christians have come to speak of Father, Son, and Holy Spirit, One God."

The sermon has well-calculated sequences and strategically worded transitional sentences. These are easily located, occurring where they should: just before the next point, and planned as a lead-in to that point.

Having given his explanation of how the Christian church came to speak of Father-Son-Spirit, Baillie expected his hearers to see the meaning of the doctrine with sharper vision. The conclusion begins, "Can you see now why I said that the doctrine of the Trinity sums up the whole Christian Gospel?" Then he launched his summary, recapitulating his three points, and moved quickly to apply the doctrine to their lives, declaring that the doctrine of the Trinity "tells you everything." "It tells you of what God is, in His external and infinite love; and of what God did in Jesus Christ for our salvation; and of what God does still today, dwelling with us as truly as He dwelt among men nineteen centuries ago, and the same forevermore."

The rest of the sermon is a call to identify with its meaning and importance, and to celebrate with the rest of the church. "So to those who know the story, the doctrine of the Trinity sums up the whole Gospel. And the Church never tires of singing in gratitude: 'Glory be to the Father, and to the Son, and to the Holy Ghost: as it was in the beginning, is now, and ever shall be, world without end.'"

A close look at how Baillie organized the elements within his message will reveal his use of both thesis (implied) and question-and-answer form. Although he stated his purpose in the third sentence of the sermon—to continue with the task of trying to understand the doctrine of the Trinity—he was most careful to keep the hearers with him in the quest with a warm invitation, "Let us try." The rest of the sermon is filled with collectives to keep the hearing occasion warm and personal; again and again the speaker used "we" and "us," wisely positing a mutual interest in an admittedly difficult endeavor.

The historical progression plan for understanding the doctrine of the Trinity demanded strategic movement through factual propositions. Baillie was persuading, or seeking to do so, without making any claim to prove his underlying thesis. He used a warm and disarming suggestion to plant the notion on which he would be working, as he confessed, "I believe we can find the whole Christian Gospel summed up in this mysterious doctrine, of three Persons, Father, Son, and Holy Spirit, in one God." He does not promise to prove it; he rather invites all the hearers to join him in a journey to search for the Gospel in that doctrine: "Let us try." He mentioned a problem and set about to solve it—with their attentive companionship. Baillie knew the path they would all take in the search to find the gospel in that doctrine; the hearers were encouraged to believe that the search would be fruitful. Baillie's "Let us try" was his sequence statement leading into the main body of the message.

G. Earl Guinn's "Resurrection of Jesus," also a doctrinal sermon, develops topically.[14] Guinn's first sentence of the introduction sets the proposition before the hearers: "The Christian religion stands or falls with the resurrection of Jesus," and the last two sentences of that introduction make an early claim upon each hearer to take the doctrine seriously: "Of the resurrection Paul had no doubts, nor should we. Faith here is crucial."

Guinn's outline is in three parts:

1. The resurrection of Jesus is indisputable history.
2. The resurrection of Jesus provides inspiring philosophy.
3. The resurrection of Jesus gives invincible hope.

The tie-in of the doctrine with the believer's life and destiny is given its strongest treatment in the last three paragraphs of the sermon. The language is celebrative and affirmative: "The Christian must not separate belief in Christ's resurrection from the confession of him as Lord. We are saved by the living Lord whom we confess and not simply by our faith in his resurrection." In so reporting, Guinn at last called upon the support of his chosen text, Romans 10:9-10, on which he had not directly relied before. Perhaps placing it last was with concern to heighten the appeal of his call to cast aside all doubt about the Resurrection fact. He had already cautioned, in his introduction, that faith in it is crucial for being Christian.

Further study of the two sermons just examined will reveal additional features in the creative design those preachers used in the interest of doctrine. In addition to these two approaches, there is still another doctrinal design in John Killinger's "There Is Still God,"[15] and there is a stronger and more overtly evangelical tone in John R. W. Stott's sermon, "I Believe in God."[16]

As one final example of a doctrinal design, you may wish to turn over to chapter 7 and examine my sermon "Death Did Not Win!" As you do so, the following questions will help you make your way into the pattern of the design.

    I. Textual-Thematic Concerns.
        1. To what use is the text put in the sermon?
        2. Is the sermon line influenced by text, by theme, or by both?
        3. What crucial aspects of the doctrine of the Resurrection are highlighted through the title?
    II. Teaching-Application Concerns
        1. What direction for faith and life are given?
        2. How is human hope clarified or renewed?

3. What "tone" is evident in the style of wording?
4. What feeling is evoked by the treatment?

BEYOND TEACHING TO ASSURANCE AND ACTION

The preacher is under trust to handle divine meanings as an official, God-sent proclaimer. The meanings come through Christian doctrine, teachings that encompass the range of human concerns and divine resources, teachings that measure life in terms of the eternal. Only such teachings have the power to grant assurance of soul and a guaranteed destiny.

Alexander Whyte (1836–1921) left a report about Bishop Joseph Butler's deathbed request. Summoning his chaplain, the dying bishop confessed: "Though I have endeavored to avoid sin and to please God to the utmost of my power; yet from the consciousness of perpetual infirmities, I am still afraid to die."

"My lord," said the chaplain, "you have forgotten that Jesus Christ is a Savior."

"True," said Butler, "but how should I know that he is a Savior for me?"

The chaplain replied, "My lord, it is written, Him that cometh to Me, I will in no wise cast out."

"True," the bishop reflected, "and I am surprised that though I have read that Scripture a thousand times over, I never felt its virtue till this moment. And now I die happy."[17]

A known teaching came alive and moved its believer into the assurance born of faith. That is the serious service of doctrine: to inform and inspire for living and dying in the will of God. Doctrine is preached with these concerns in view.

Arthur John Gossip (1873–1954), lecturing to some ministers about the place of biblical doctrine in preaching, encouraged them to do more and more to inform their hearers about the whole counsel of God. He forthrightly stated, "Multitudes have found the doctrines, so far from being useless and cumbersome, a first necessity and the very breath of life to them; so far from being tedious and boring, beyond all computation, more thrilling and exciting than anything else in the round world."[18] Such encouragement bids the preacher strive for excellence as a doctrinal preacher, working always to carry hearers beyond teaching to belief, assurance, and right action.

V. DESIGNING THE FUNERAL SERMON

The preacher is charged with the need to speak a word from the Lord, and never is that necessity so crucial as when death invades the family or church circle and a word must be set beside the experience for all those involved in feeling it. The sermon is an important vehicle of meaning at such a time. It is a strategic way to focus faith and release feeling. It mediates meaning and conveys a sense of presence. But an extra degree of intensity is usually involved in funeral preaching, and the affective tones of the preacher's words are much higher than at any other time. A part of this relates to a deepened human concern to gain something more from the sermon under conditions of felt loss and bereavement.

THE RITUAL CONTEXT OF FUNERALS

There are certain ritual conventions that the preacher is expected to know and honor where funerals are concerned. So much of what is said and done carries a sign-value. The effects of certain colors are subtle and profound. The pace at which the service moves makes its declaration about what is being done, and that pace communicates a mood; some will sense it all as a special time *(kairos)*, and others will see it all in connection with ongoing life *(chronos)*. But over the whole context of the funeral service hangs a cloud of meaning that waters the experience of death and helps people grow in faith and understanding about God's ways with man.

The rituals associated with the service are part of the long view of life by which meanings are preserved and passed on from one generation to another. Spoken and acted rituals do capture the past, but they do more. They make meanings concrete, giving them a present tense so that we can comprehend those meanings in ever fresh ways. Special times and special places only deepen our awareness of the meanings, and sharing with one another at those times and in those special places generates a sense of community among those who gather in common.

Regarding the funeral sermon, the preacher has four main options as the design is shaped: (1) to treat the meaning of the experience of death; (2) to comfort the bereaved family and friends; or (3) to treat the life and work of the deceased person, delivering a eulogy about the dead loved one. The next option (4) involves a mix of the previous three, since funerals do involve those who need comfort, those who need a fresh word about life and death, and the need to say something about the life of the one whose parting made the occasion necessary. But usually one of the first three options will be given a major place in the sermon design, and the ritual expectations related to the occasion can help the preacher in planning and handling the preaching task.

SOME GUIDELINES FOR THE FUNERAL SERMON DESIGN

1. *Determine the major focus of the sermon in keeping with the conditions surrounding the person's death.* The direction one should follow in preaching is often sensed while studying the event of the person's passing.

Death is a part of the rhythm of life, the end result of a

combination of factors, and the preacher can wisely highlight the attitude the person had while facing death, or the person's courage in the fight against some disease that worked away at his strength, thus affirming that person's handling of life in a way that helps those who are left behind.

The preacher might well choose to speak about the "rest" into which faithful believers enter at death, or point with confidence and gracious bearing to the goodness and mercy of God extended to all his children.

The focus of the sermon must be determined with care, and the preacher's words must be honest and apt. Funerals make us face the profound dimensions of reality, and every proven resource should be called upon to help us shape our words with care: biblical wisdom, folk culture, and the home circle. It is largely in the preacher's hands to help the living find deeper spiritual meaning when life is upset and invaded by the fact of some loved one's death.

2. *Plan the language in keeping with the sermon focus.* There will be times when the language of lament will be in order, lament that the deceased person will no longer be with us in our work and group life. Those who lament will want to review that person's contribution to the group, and the preacher will be expected to call attention to essential facts and strategic details. The lament will thus have a personal tone and convey a sense of intimacy with the one whose life is being honored.

There are times when the language of praise must be used, praise spoken for a well-spent life of faith and service. But the mix of lament and praise is seldom an easy accomplishment, and the stress will ordinarily be on the one or the other. But again, the conditions of the person's death will help the preacher to see the whole scene and find a proper focus.

This is why funeral sermons are usually entrusted to those who have known the deceased person, or, lacking that acquaintance, who had had considerable experience in handling emotion-ridden occasions. Seldom is a funeral sermon left to someone who is a total stranger to the bereaved family or the community in which the deceased lived. When this happens, so much can go wrong.

Howard Thurman tells of being seven years old when his father died, and he has never fogotten the trauma he experienced when the guest preacher delivered a funeral sermon that did violence to his memory of his father. That guest preacher handling the funeral had not known Saul Thurman. Yet that preacher dared to assess Saul Thurman's nonmembership in the local church the family attended as evidence that he was a nonbeliever, and he forthrightly declared him lost and in hell. That preacher wanted to make the occasion an object lesson for all who were "outside the church."

As young Howard sat on the mourner's seat, he kept saying to his mother beside him, "He didn't know Pappa? Did he? Did he, Momma?"[1] Alice Thurman, Howard's mother, held her calm through the service and gently patted her son's knees to comfort him as the verbal violence ate away at his young mind and spirit. It was the handling of that sermon by that preacher, Thurman tells us, that turned him against the church for awhile during his youth. Lacking intimacy with the family, that preacher would have been wiser and more helpful if he had chosen to comfort the family rather than interpret the life of the deceased.

Having mentioned doing violence to the memory of the deceased, there are several stories about how John Jasper (1812–1901) used to do this. That legendary black pulpit giant "was preeminently a funeral preacher," we are told,[2] and there are several sermons preserved from his ministry on such occasions.

One story about John Jasper concerns a combined funeral occasion for two persons, one William Ellyson and one Mary Barnes. The preacher was rather blunt in treating the memory of

Ellyson. He reminded the hearers that the man had not lived as a good man, that he had died without God and without hope, adding, in his heavy dialect, "It's a bad tale to tell on 'im, but he fix de story hissef." Then he warned the hearers that a funeral must be according to the life of the departed.

But the eulogy for Mary Barnes was a noble statement of praise about her life in faith. Jasper declared, "I know'd her."[3] His sermon honoring her life is filled with the language of praise and epitaphs drawn from the Bible he loved to use in all his preaching. His sermon was a verbal compliment, addressed as if to her, an official interpretation of what her life meant to all the faithful ones in the church to which she belonged and in which she had loyally worked across the years. So much comes through in the preacher-pastor's declaration, "I know'd her." It was a thankful pastor's final moment to celebrate a member. Given the right conditions, all attending members expect such a statement from the one who designs and delivers the funeral sermon.

The language ritual in the funeral sermon should be truthful, resourceful, tasteful, intimate, consoling, economical in wording, and emotionally controlled.

3. *Whenever possible, plan the sermon on the level of the heroic.* This will enable those who grieve to express their grief with understood pride and social solace.

In speaking about the level of the heroic, I am referring to the way a sermon can be a ritual victory over death. It can speak to the issue of finality by speaking words that put the dead to rest in the mind of the mourners. In the black church tradition in which I was nurtured, this was done as the preacher would "pull the sting out" of death by reciting the resurrection story. John Jasper was doing this when, in that same sermon over Mary Barnes, he bent over slightly, put his hand to his mouth in megaphone fashion, and cried out to challenge death: "Grave! Grave! O Grave! Where is your victory?" He was in a ritual recitation against death, celebrating the power of Jesus over death, and was thereby helping the mourners and hearers to reaffirm their faith, hope, and confidence in their own destiny as believers. Great power lies in heroic rhetoric, and that power should be invoked by the preacher whenever the circumstances allow and warrant it.

Dr. Benjamin E. Mays was working at the heroic level in his euology honoring the late Dr. Martin Luther King, Jr.[4] Mays dealt with a mixture of concerns on that occasion. He treated the meaning of King's life and ministry, the nature of prophetic service, and the tension everybody was feeling because the assassin had not yet been caught. That eulogy also called upon all to help finish King's unfinished work. The circumstances surrounding the slain leader's death demanded that heroic approach. And Dr. May's intimate friendship with the younger King gave a personal tone to the eulogy that was authentic and appealing. It helped the speaker to shape the experience of hearing into an enduring monument of meaning and honor. A leader was being interpreted by a leader. A great spokesman was honoring a great spokesman. An activist was being credited by an activist. Meaning was being boldly formalized for all, and grief was being lanced so that deep feelings could bleed under controlled conditions.

Writer James Baldwin has told about the funeral of his father in 1943. Although they were blood father and son, the two did not know each other very well. The father had been a kind of recluse, and his son had grown up fearing to be in his presence. That father had also been a bitter man, bitter because of the many boundaries he had known as a black man in hostile white surroundings. Nevertheless, during the funeral, the preacher— a long-time friend of the father, spoke of Baldwin's dad as "thoughtful, patient, and forbearing, a Christian inspiration to all who knew him, and a model for his children."[5] As Baldwin thought back on it all, he reasoned that the preacher was dealing with the issues at a level deeper than questions of fact, so involved was he in his friend's life that *this* interpretation was the dead man's life and that it must by all means be known by all. So Baldwin added,

> Every man in the chapel hoped that when his hour came he, too, would be eulogized, which is to say, forgiven, and that all of his lapses, greeds, errors, and strayings from the truth would be invested with coherence and looked upon with charity. This was perhaps the last thing human beings could give each other and it was what they demanded, after all, of the Lord.

Some time ago I chanced upon a television special on dying. The program was pulled from a two-year study in which three persons facing death shared their reactions as they waited for the end. All three persons struggled to remain calm while waiting on death. Open talk took place to help the marriage partner understand how death would involve him or her. But one of the most moving episodes involved an elderly black man, a minister, who was dying of cancer. Told that no cure was available, he decisively stated: "I'm not gonna die on account of death." He preached a brief personal statement about death and then returned South to be with his family. He wanted to take a last look around at familiar faces and long-loved places. When he died, it was with dignity, with his grandchildren playing beside his bed.

He had not wanted a spectacle. He wanted the drama of the end to be lived in that home setting. This was his way of helping the family deal with raw fact, and to do so in shameless affirmation that death belongs to God even as life belongs to him. He wanted to have a meaningful homegoing.

A newswriter also saw that special program and published some interesting comments about the black man's death-setting. "Through this black minister," he wrote, "dying is seen as an act of fundamental faith, a tribute to the necessary illusion

that gives man a final identity."[6] The writer marveled at the
backward leap that minister had taken just because of his
forward faith.

It is this that is affirmed through heroic sermons over the
dead. It is what Howard Thurman referred to as "going down to
one's grave with a *shout*."[7]

It is with this in mind that the language of the sermon must be
planned. And it is why the language of the church must be used
at strategic points in the sermon. There is special import in the
mention of such words as "grace," "deliverance," "hope,"
"faith," "forgiveness," "love," "eternal life," "peace," "assurance." The sermon must be planned with affective meanings in
mind for the hearers.

In summary, the funeral sermon should be designed with the
major focus well-set: namely, to treat the meaning of death in
human experience, or to comfort the bereaved, or to honor the
life of the deceased, or to do a bit of each of these where
necessary. The best direction to follow is usually sensed as one
studies the eventful elements associated with someone's death.
The language of the sermon must match the sermon focus, so
that lament or praise, or both, can help the hearers to relate well
to the occasion as sharers under the preacher's clear guidance.
Whenever possible, the sermon should be planned and
delivered on the heroic level. It should give the mourners some
sense of pride in the midst of their loss and bereavement.

VI. STUDYING THE METHODS
OF MASTER PREACHERS

Suggestive help toward designing sermons for increased effectiveness is readily available if one reads widely among preaching theorists and studies deeply among master sermons. Both ancient and contemporary textbooks and monographs can contribute much to our understanding of preaching styles, help us to assess preaching trends, and aid us in locating ourselves with respect to our own personal gifts and inclinations for pulpit work.

Those who desire to handle preaching in an able manner need to act and react responsibly with respect to theories about our work, on the one hand, while watching live models at work, on the other. This chapter will list some of the benefits one can gain by studying the master preachers. The major focus here will be upon the sermons of pulpit masters.

THEORIZING FROM LIFE

Andrew W. Blackwood (1882–1966), noted teacher of preaching and preachers, commented that "the man who would learn how to preach may approach the subject in one of three ways, . . . the science of homiletics, the art of preaching, and the study of sermons."[1] The person concerned to preach well will approach the subject in all three ways, learning from theory, from personal experience, and from direct observation. As for observation, it helps to balance and correct theory since it lets us see and learn from what actually happens or happened. Theorizing from life helps preachers gain perspective on what is intensely practical; it also encourages us to appreciate and develop what is genuinely personal. The preparation and delivery of sermons must be both practical and personal. All help, therefore, to be authentically personal and to do what is distinctly practical is to our good. Studying master preachers and their work aids us greatly in this way.

One can well begin by surveying a list of acknowledged pulpit masters in order to choose someone for prolonged and detailed study. The most extensive list now available appears in *Twenty Centuries of Great Preaching*, an encyclopedia set of thirteen volumes, edited by Clyde E. Fant, Jr., and William M. Pinson, Jr. [2] The entire set of volumes treats preachers and preaching, over ninety acknowledged masters, with representative sermons for examining their pulpit work. The set covers most of the centuries of church history, from the apostolic era down to the 1970s. Each preacher selected for study has been discussed in a concise biography, together with an analysis of his preaching and a sampling of sermons that reflect style, substance, and design. Perusing the list of preachers treated in the set, a student will surely come across certain names that will challenge interest as figures for study. Those who take the time to do that study will discover deeper levels of appreciation for our task opening within themselves; they will also discover fresh insights and encouragement for working harder to achieve a more able workmanship in sermon design and delivery.

There are still other books that list able preachers whose work is worthy of study. One thinks about the noted list of men who have given the Lyman Beecher Lectures on Preaching at Yale, [3] and the Warrack Lectures in Scotland.[4] Guidance is also available in histories of preaching (general, denominational, and so on). The best listing for the twentieth century has been supplied in A *History of Preaching,* volume 3, prepared by Ralph C. Turnbull to continue the work left unfinished by Edwin C. Dargan when he died. Historian Horton Davies has treated the contemporary British preaching scene in his *Varieties of English Preaching: 1900–1960;* he offers an in-depth study of selected English preachers and their sermonic work.[5]

The suggestions given here for finding a preacher (or preachers) and sermons for study form but a partial list, but certainly a central one. After surveying such listings the student can move on to enlarge the range of choice through suggestions from others, or from personal reading, and experiences of hearing sermons of striking substance and effectiveness. All considered, the purpose behind choosing some pulpit master for study is to gain insight into the work and discover methods that can teach us more sermon effectiveness through sensed dimension and design.

FROM ONE PREACHER TO ANOTHER

1. *Great sermons usually reflect a preacher's concern for his or her task and times.* It is of great importance to trace this concern as it stands revealed in someone's preaching. The sermons of Helmut Thielicke, for instance, or those of Martin Luther King, Jr. (1929–1968), especially the latter's sermon "Antidotes for Fear,"[6] take on increased meaning and depth when one recalls the state of the times and what was happening in their lives when the sermons were preached. Both men preached constantly under the threat of death, Thielicke facing the imminent fact of death due to war and bombing raids upon Germany, and King

facing death at the hands of obstructionists opposed to granting civil rights.

Some sermons are best studied in connection with information about the time, and place preached. Blackwood rightly pointed out that "the state of the times affects the substance and the tone color of every sermon."[7] Great sermons usually reflect the preacher's understanding and concern for the people who heard them, the scene of their lives, and the spirit of their times.

2. *Sermons worthy of study also reveal how the preacher's personality influenced the preaching style.* The classic statement by Phillips Brooks (1835–1893) that "preaching is the communication of truth by man to men,"[8] usually shortened into "truth through personality," keeps us reminded that a sermon is more than a speech, that it is flavored by a life and reddened by human blood, with all that this implies. The cast of a sermon reveals the mold of the speaker's life and mind, his or her faith and levels of feeling. There are times when this can be a problem, to be sure; but under the right circumstances this becomes an added dimension of sermon power and appeal.

3. *Studying sermons preached by others allows us to trace out how the preacher related words and the Word.* In true preaching so much turns upon the use of biblical substance and the kerygmatic witness, as we have seen. The sermon also allows us to sense some possible echo of the note of worship since preaching is a part of the preacher's praise of God.

This understanding of the sermon as an act of worship has influenced many preachers as to sermon design, tone, wording, and tie-in with other elements in the worship service. It has also made some preachers have deep misgivings about publishing their sermons since, as George Arthur Buttrick so rightly explained, "the congregation 'makes' the sermon almost as much as the preacher makes it," adding, "Remove the prayer-worship, the brooding of the Spirit on the worshiping congregation, and how much of the sermon is left? A sermon is an 'offering' on an altar.'"[9]

While it is true that it takes an understanding of a sermon in its worship setting to sense its full flavor, there is still much that its words indicate and evidence even beyond that setting. The student can surely trace out how the sermon relates to the biblical tradition, whether the preacher's sermon-statement is biblically grounded at all points.

Before leaving this matter of the preacher's words, something more needs to be mentioned concerning it. Sermon design proceeds by an intentional use of words. It involves words at the level of sound effects (pitch, phrasing, pausing), at the level of vision and meaning (vocabulary), all under basic control and strict choice. Worthy sermons all reflect strategic word usage on the part of the preacher, so the student should spend a generous amount of time examining what words were used and what effects were intended in that use. Most of the great preachers have been word artists, using the language of the people with greater skill than most. As John Masefield once explained, "The great man holds what his race holds and makes a splendid use of it; he does supremely what all are doing about him in some measure." No small part of studying someone's sermon is the examination of their choice and use of words.

It is also well to remember that those whose word-patterns prove to be exemplary are not necessarily persons who always had a unique gift for words, or who operated always out of an instinct for speaking with aptness. Many of the great preachers have confessed how hard they worked at using the language well. Their skills in using words were hard-won; they gained aptness and effectiveness by constant vigilance and persistent effort. It is possible to trace that pattern of growth on their part by comparing sermons from the periods of a preacher's life, if such sermons are available. In instance upon instance one will be able to see the preacher's progress: the later sermons showing a more ear-directed quality, with the word-flow designed and controlled to effect directness, betray immediacy, and guarantee an economical use of pulpit time.[10]

Whatever the preacher's giftedness and level of development as a word-craftsman, there is nothing more exhilarating in the study of a sermon than to *feel* the power and rhythm of its lines. There is something extremely pleasurable in exemplary speech-forms and sound patterns. Growing up in a setting where vocal expressiveness was both cultivated and appreciated, especially at high levels of pulpit work, I speak personally and with warmth about what studying the sermons of some masters has meant to my life and learning. There is a richness and relevance in excellent word-usage harnessed in the service of the Lord. And when with honest toil and spiritual concern a sermon is shaped and so used, an immediacy and whole-person approach attends it. To study such a sermon is to sense the life that seeks always to break through words.

A FEW CAUTIONS

It is necessary at this point to raise three cautions in connection with the studying of great sermons: (1) resist the temptation to feel inferior in the presence of greatness; (2) resist the temptation to re-use someone's sermon after you have been impressed by it; (3) resist the temptation to rank preachers in terms of which one is the proverbial "best."

Sermons with apparent insight, careful design, and ardent expressiveness have a way of quieting us, making us look again and again at ourselves with the searching eyes of one who laments, "Will *I* ever . . . ?" However thoughtful any preacher's sermon design might make us, whatever instructions for improvement we hear speaking to us in the workmanship, we should not let the apparent prowess of another stunt our own sense of worth as a worker under God. Worthy models and designs created by others should encourage us to work harder at it, and with surer aim and vision. Every true preacher has strengths and limitations. We study one another to find help; we need not leave that study filled with despair. Let no one walk away from the study of some great sermon bent over in self-pity, crushed under the weight of the shadow of some pulpit giant.

Great sermons by others not only provide a humbling measure against which to test our own level of achievement, but they can intimidate our spirit of creativity so that one despairs of ever dealing with a given text or topic—unless by using a master's sermon, either in part or in whole. There is, however, another way to benefit personally from the prowess and planning of another preacher: one can attempt viewing a text or topic as through his or her mind's eye, and stimulate one's own mind to consider aspects and angles that might not otherwise be considered. In this way, the style of another preacher will help us to reflect, priming our own pump, as it were, until the mental juices flow with steadiness and strength.

John Henry Jowett (1864–1923), a preacher of exceptional talent, tells us that he quite often did this. Working alone in his study, poring over some text in order to gather its treasures, Jowett would try looking at the text after the manner of other preachers with whose mind and style he was familiar. "I ask, —how would Newman regard this subject? How would Spurgeon approach it? How would Dale deal with it? By what road would Bushnell come up to it? Where would Maclaren take his stand to look at it? Where would Alexander Whyte lay hold on it?"[11] This way of proceeding broadened and enriched Jowett's thinking as he viewed a text or topic. He honestly faced the fact that his own mind, unaided, would naturally miss aspects of thought until other minds helped to point them out and make him aware of them. Jowett could use this method, however, because he had studied the sermons of these thought-provoking preachers; he knew their methods of work and sermon design. He learned from them and enhanced his own gifts. Watching others and learning from them should help us find release to do our best work. No study of what others have done should leave us imprisoned in their greatness, victims of their shadowing strengths, and lacking the will to discover what excellencies might be in our selves.

Gardner C. Taylor, celebrated Brooklyn pastor, accented the positive benefits that should follow the study of another's pulpit work. "Any preacher greatly deprives himself or herself who does not study the recognized masters of pulpit discourse, not to copy them but rather to see what has been the way in which they approached the Scriptures, their craftsmanship, their feel for men's hearts."[12] Himself a preacher of world renown, Taylor paid tribute in his 1976 Beecher Lectures to several preachers whose work had taught and stimulated him, among them Paul E. Scherer (1892–1969), Arthur John Gossip (1873–1954), and F. W. Boreham (1871–1959).[13] Much from each man's work stands available in print, and each one's gift for metaphor and shapely thought shows the excellence of his craftsmanship and the depths in his sermon substance. Gardner Taylor's own pulpit gifts are unusual and highly instructive. Few preachers can handle his penchant for long sentences so well, showing lights and shadows by such ready adjectives, pictorial phrases, and the traditional grand manner of euphony and resonance. One can learn so much about preaching through the exemplary work of this contemporary.[14]

And now a word about that third caution, which was to avoid making hard lines of rank among preachers and sermons. It is the work and purpose of preaching that we must exalt, not the workmen. We can learn from the various methods of men without idolizing either methods or men. In final fact, sermons are great which accomplish their aim, when the message is so handled as to be openly heard, fully accepted, and readily obeyed. Perhaps there is no *best* among preachers, but rather as Paul once put it, "different kinds of gifts, but the same Spirit . . . different kinds of service, but the same Lord, . . . different kinds of working, but the same God works all of them in all men" (I Cor. 12:4-6, NIV). It is far wiser to honor individual distinctiveness than to attempt ranking preachers as to which one or ones are the greatest.

The wisdom of honoring individual distinctives among those who preach becomes clear as one traces the different approaches preachers take in handling the same text. Every other year I teach a graduate course for seminarians on the methods of master preachers. The members of the class are guided in studying some outstanding preacher and his pulpit work. The concern is to examine the preacher's work to discover his or her source of power, methods, and the individual skills and insights utilized to meet the spiritual needs of his or her times. Among the many discoveries such studies allow, the seminarians are usually impressed most by the lack of duplication among master preachers in gifts, approaches, and skills in serving.

I remember assigning several students to study the treatment a select number of preachers had made of the same text. In one instance two students reported on the difference of treatment given to John 7:17 between Frederick William Robertson (1816–1853) and Joseph Fort Newton (1880–1950). Robertson's topic was "Obedience, the Organ of Spiritual Knowledge,"[15] and Newton's was in question form, "How Do We Know in Religion?"[16] Robertson treated the text in his characteristic two-part contrast fashion, his philosophical bent always to the fore, while Newton's outline was not as evident but his poetic statement was illuminating nevertheless.

In another instance two students contrasted the treatment given to John 10:14-15 by Robertson and that given by Leslie D.

Weatherhead (1893–1976). Both preachers used the same topic, "The Good Shepherd," with Weatherhead using a four-point outline, while Robertson had followed his usual two-point arrangement.[17]

In still another instance of choice, one student studied Alexander Whyte's (1836–1921) sermon "To the Uttermost," based on Hebrews 7:25; and another student examined John Albert Broadus' (1827–1895) treatment of that text in his sermon "He Ever Liveth to Intercede."[18] Whyte centered attention upon the results and extent of our salvation; Broadus delved more fully into the person of Jesus as Savior and Intercessor.

Other choices and distinctions were traced between John Henry Jowett's handling of Ephesians 3:8 (topic: "The Disciples' Theme") and Clarence Edward Macartney's (1879–1957) treatment of the same text (topic: "The Unsearchable Riches of Christ").[19] There was also considerable contrast between the way Macartney handled Genesis 45:27 in his sermon "When Jacob Saw the Wagons,"[20] and the way Robert B. Whyte treated it in his sermon "Intimations of an Unseen Helper."[21] Both men tried to span the testaments and called attention to the meaning of Christ, but in each case the style was the man, making each sermon bear the special marks of individual distinctives peculiar to the unique workman. Sermon structures varied because aims differed, as did each preacher's way with a text.

GUIDELINES FOR STUDYING SERMONS

The following lines of approach to a sermon will help the student to go about the task of study with some sense of good direction. It is assumed here that the student will use these guidelines primarily while working with written sermons, but the lines of approach apply as well to the study of sermons on tapes and discs from live preaching situations. It should also be understood that so much is missing from a sermon when one has only the written text to use—the preacher's voice is not heard, so one misses its qualities, the rate of speech, and other aspects of "presence." There is the advantage, however, of seeing what was said when a written sermon text is available, and the student can read and reread the lines at his or her own pace.

1. In preparing to examine a sermon, read it through *aloud* to gain an "inside feel" of its message, tone, and thrust.

2. Locate the preacher's central aim or objective. How is that objective stated? Is it open or hidden?

3. Locate the sermon outline and mark the major points. Does the topic (or subject) of the sermon relate well to that outline? Does the order of the points show logical sequence? How is that sequence made to grip and guide the hearer? What motivating techniques does the preacher employ in holding the hearer's attention? How apt was the *introduction* as a "door opener" for the sermon thesis?

4. Trace the relationship between the sermon and its text. In what ways is the biblical message stated or reflected in the sermon outline? Is the text the preacher's main authority or an auxiliary aid? What unstated assumptions come through to you about the preacher's view of scripture?

5. How does the preacher handle facts in his message? How complete is his or her information? How engaging is the treatment of the sermon's real intention? Do the preacher's judgments reflect care for the right to be heard? What convictions are voiced—and how are they stated?

6. How is the central idea illustrated? Are the illustrations literary, colloquial, or personal? Are they hackneyed or fresh? In what ways does the preacher repeat the idea for the emphasis and clarity?

7. Examine the preacher's vocabulary level. Are the words of the sermon colloquial or professional, popular or literary,

or mixed? Are the sentences simple or compound or mixed?

8. What personal tone comes through in the sermon? Does that personal tone convey warmth, understanding, and caring on the part of the preacher?

9. Think of the text and topic of the sermon in relation to your own church or place of worship: How would its message be heard by those whom you know and serve? If you used that text or topic, what modifications would need to be made in the sermon design to ready it for that different set of listeners? How would your introduction differ? How would your understanding of the text differ? How would your illustrations, wording, and application of the sermon differ?

10. Write down what the sermon taught you about textual interpretation; sermon unity; the ordering of the idea elements; sentencing for description, clarity, and movement; applying the sermon insight; method of concluding.

11. Go back through the sermon and isolate statements you may want to use as quotations in another setting. Be careful to make full documentation as you add the quotable materials to your files.

THE BASIC OBJECTIVE REVIEWED

Helmut Thielicke, acclaimed German preacher-theologian, has written about his long-time admiration for the pulpit ministry of Charles Haddon Spurgeon (1834–1892). The facts of Spurgeon's exemplary pulpit work made Thielicke take bold notice: six thousand persons came to hear him preach every Sunday; his sermons were cabled to New York every Monday and reprinted in the leading American newspapers; the man preached from his pulpit for almost forty years without losing his appeal, without repetition, and without going dry. The miracle of it all challenged Thielicke to study the man and his ministry, especially in relation to the man's times.

After prolonged study of Spurgeon, Thielicke wrote,

> I am almost tempted to shout out to those who are serving the eternal Word as preachers, and to those who are preparing to do so, in what I hope will be a productive hyperbole: Sell all that you have (not least of all some of your stock of current sermonic literature) and buy Spurgeon (even if you have to grub through the second-hand bookstores).[22]

Then, referring the reader on to that section of his book made up of excerpts selected from Spurgeon's lectures to his many students, Thielicke further advised: "Use this seminar of his, to which you are here invited, not as a mere drill that will train you to homiletical perfection, but rather as an exercise in which you come to yourself and find your 'own individual tone.' "

Yes, that is it. That is the grand and fruitful goal of the study one makes of the master preachers—to find one's own individual tone and intended effectiveness.

Donald E. Demaray closes his illuminating book *Pulpit Giants* with some summary statements about the major characteristics held in common by the twenty-six master preachers he has discussed.[23] Among those characteristics Demaray listed were these:

a) an utter seriousness about the call to preach
b) a passion to communicate
c) a readiness to be individual
d) an eagerness to study, learn, and use the learning
e) a sensitive concern for persons
f) an ability to concentrate meaningfully and faithfully on their given task

g) a healthy discontent with their own spiritual progress and ministerial success

h) an honorable view of preaching as the most important activity in which they could be involved.

There were other suggested characteristics held in common by the great pulpit masters, but those listed above provide a quite high and clear mark for all to reach who seek to fulfill the high calling of God to preach.

VII. THREE ILLUSTRATED DESIGNS

SERMON STYLE 1. NARRATIVE/STORY

Anatomy of a Failure

But the thing that David had done displeased the Lord.
— II Samuel 11:27*b*

I

It was springtime in the Holy Land. It was that season of the year when military campaigns were normally undertaken. The rains were just over, and the hovering fog of winter had now dispersed. Nature was stirring itself in newness, and Israel's armies had gone forth to quell trouble from the marauding Ammonites. Civil strife in the land made that springtime a less enjoyable one.

David especially felt the pressures from it all, so he did not go out at the head of the troops this time. Wearied by recent warfare against the Syrians, David sent General Joab to head Israel's forces. As king, David remained behind in Jerusalem. This choice was unfortunate, and II Samuel 11 tells us why. That chapter reports something King David did that displeased the Lord. So dastardly was his deed that it had repercussions down through the years, not only in David's own life but in his family and in the nation over which he was king.

II

It happened late one afternoon. David arose from his couch and walked up on the roof of his house, no doubt thinking as he walked. A king's business demands thought, much thought, and David needed time to think with care.

But as David walked and thought, as he paced and pondered, he let his eyes linger on a scene from which he should have turned away. From his high roof he could see down into the courtyard of a nearby house, and he noticed a woman there bathing herself.

The affairs of state were slowly pushed aside as David let his eyes linger on what should have remained a neighbor's privacy. Steadily peering beyond his balcony, David finally set his eyes in a lust-influenced stare. Casting aside the propriety one would expect from a godly king, or a concerned gentleman, or a caring neighbor, David let his feeling become inflamed. It was not long before a lawless deed was in the making.

The first stage of a moral failure had occurred. The last stages would be worse than the first; adultery, a pregnancy, an attempted cover-up that did not succeed, and the murder of the woman's legal husband.

If only David had not decided to rest himself from war that spring! If only he had gone out to do battle as before!

But there are times when one breaks a pattern. There are those times when one needs a break in the midst of some routine. There are those times when one decides to withdraw for thought. There are those times when one decides to let someone else handle a matter during a desired or necessary absence.

The full problem with David's failure was not in where he was, nor when he was there, but what he did with himself while there. That restful rooftop could have become a place of needed insight; it did not have to become a scene of sensual planning. David's failure cannot be charged to his being in Jerusalem and up on his roof. That failure must be charged to David's selfishness of mind and sinfulness of heart.

III

David did not have to keep looking across his balcony into his neighbor's courtyard. And he should not have kept looking. That inner court was a private spot for the family that lived there. Open to the sky, perhaps tiled, that courtyard had a cistern and drainage system that made bathing convenient. It was secluded from the street and was a haven to family members seeking privacy from the outside world.

David broke the code of neighborliness through his prolonged stare. David defied the ethics of privacy. Worse still, he broke the law of God by his lustful longing. His surprised first glance did not have to become an unsettling stare. But that king let lust do its work in him, and a failure nurtured by fantasy was on the way.

Thomas a Kempis explained it clearly when he wrote: "For first there cometh to the mind a bare thought of evil, then a strong imagination thereof, afterward delight and evil motion, and consent." Fantasy always plays its part in this kind of failure. Fantasy stirs imagination; imagination excites anticipation; anticipation prompts planning; and decisive action follows with selfishly appropriate timing.

It would have been better that David be wounded in battle than have his soul scarred by such sins! Far better that his own life be lost in the war than that he become murderer in an attempted cover-up for his sorry and ill-fated deed!

IV

It is no small matter to displease the Lord. There was nothing casual about violating another home, disregarding the woman's husband, and selfishly claiming Bathsheba in defiance of all God commanded for the nation's good. David displeased the Lord. He acted selfishly in lust. He was king, but what he was did not rightly influence what he did. Here is a sad lesson in the lack of self-management.

David displeased the Lord. He failed to resist temptation. He failed to be a godly neighbor and respect his neighbor's rights. He acted loosely although he held high office. He dared to act high-handedly, even as a despot, trying to cover his dirty tracks through the murder of an innocent husband—a man who was his neighbor and a loyal soldier in his army!

David displeased the Lord. He deified his own lusts. He misused his leisure. He defied God's laws. David failed not by accident but by choice. How could he have believed the sad failure was worth it? Failure is never worth the success. It is never a good deed if what is done displeases the Lord.

V

Make no mistake about it: There are some things that displease the Lord.

There are those in our time who say that they care nothing about what the Bible holds up as proper standards for living and behavior. There are so many in our world who confess no strict sense of accountability to God or to family or to nation or to humankind. For them, personal preferences are absolute; and they follow these, and these alone. Their morality is whatever they feel to do; their goal is to please themselves.

There are others in our time who say that they do know about God, who say that they are taught from the Bible about life and living; and they openly confess that their conscience reacts before and after a deed. They admit that they know what pleases the Lord and what displeases him, and they acknowledge faith that there are meanings beyond themselves, meanings by which their days are measured.

David was one who knew better. He sinned with an informed mind. And his guilt afterward was heavier than the affairs of state could ever be! Displeasing the Lord is never a small matter, a slight affair, a casual happening, a mere passing event. The deed that displeases God jars the life. It scars the soul. It darkens the mind. It unsettles the nerves. It poisons the body. It enthrones self. It ruins the future. It invites divine judgment. The things that displease the Lord destroy us if we persist in them.

The prophet Nathan confronted David about his sin. Nathan reminded the king of the many trusts he had violated. The king was guilty but honest and repentant about it all; he did not resist the prophetic word of rebuke and censure. David confessed. He was forgiven, and he accepted the judgment of God deemed appropriate in his case.

VI

This story of David carries a heavy message. It warns us all to exercise care about how we live. It reminds us that security against displeasing God lies in loving God more than we love ourselves. But David's story tells us still more: It tells us that sin, however great and gross, can be forgiven if we are truly sorry over it.

Failure is failure, yes! But it does not have to remain unforgiven. David did reap sad consequences from his sin, yes! But once forgiven, he had the Lord's mercies to aid him as he lived with those sad effects. Being back in the Lord's favor made all the difference for David. It is the same for any and all of us now, whatever our failure has been.

SERMON STYLE 2. TEXTUAL/EXPOSITORY

He Was Faithful

He was faithful to him who appointed him, just as Moses also was faithful in God's house.
                                        —Hebrews 3:2

Dr. George A. Buttrick, the noted New York pastor, was asked to prepare a short biography of Jesus for a secular magazine. The editor asked that the article be no longer than a thousand words. Buttrick confessed that he was greatly exercised about what to omit and what to include; it was deeply disturbing to have to decide about what was uniquely important.[1] My text is a still shorter description of Jesus, but its highly selective wording immediately pinpoints a most vital statistic about him: "He was faithful to him who appointed him" (Heb. 3:2). The writer's tribute about Jesus honors our Lord's life, but it is also a measure against which we should test our response to God's will for us. Let us examine this matter of faithfulness to God, watching Jesus' life in order rightly to shape our own.

I

Faithfulness to God was a needed subject for those who first received our text. Those readers were being tested by life; they were under growing persecution from hostile unbelievers. Some of them were weakening in faith and becoming confused about the Christian way. Offended by calculated persecution and weakened by selfish concern, some others had already turned from following Jesus. Thus the Letter to the Hebrews and its message about the faith and faithfulness of Jesus.

The subject of faithfulness is important for us in this our time. We too need to follow Jesus more attentively. Caught up, as so many are, in a society whose life and morale depend upon more and more movement, and whose mind-set is upon more and more things, we need to remind one another about the deeper issues of what it means to live. We too need to remember that we are never so successful as when, like Jesus, we live obediently and joyfully in faithfulness to God, "under orders," as it were. I speak of "orders" with purpose because faithfulness to God involves an obedient response to a known role or assignment.

Jesus knew his "orders" and he carried them out cheerfully, with alertness and singleness of heart. The Gospels tell us again and again that Jesus knew himself as one on assignment for God: "The Spirit of the Lord is upon me. . . . He has sent me . . . (Luke 4:18); "I must preach the good news of the kingdom of God to the other cities also; for I was sent for this purpose" (Luke 4:43); "My food is to do the will of him who sent me; and to accomplish his work" (John 4:34); "For this I was born, and for this I have come into the world, to bear witness to the truth" (John 18:37b). Jesus knew that he was under orders, God's orders for his life. Our text commends his response: he was faithful to God.

The Letter to the Hebrews adds to what the Gospels tell us and supplies rich detail about his orders from God. The writer refers to Jesus as "the apostle and high priest of our confession" (3:1). This phrasing is unique to this writer, and it points to a specific service Jesus renders in our behalf. As "apostle," all initiative for what Jesus did lay in the hands of God who sent him; as "high priest," Jesus could ably speak to God for us and as one of us. His preparation to be an apostle and high priest was prolonged and perilous as he walked the road of life with us. It meant being involved in situations of demand and decision. It meant surrendering to God's will. Jesus did it. He proved true to what God asked of him. The text declares: "He was faithful to him who appointed him." Jesus did not have an easy way in his obedience, but that is why we commend him all the more.

II

Convinced that his life-wearied readers needed to sense the meaning of Jesus' faithfulness, the writer went on to compare him to Moses, that well-honored pioneer figure. He wrote: "Jesus was faithful to him who appointed him, *just as Moses* also was faithful in God's house."

The readers knew and revered the story of Moses. His life and times stood high in their thinking and regard. They knew that Moses' ministry had brought a major turning point in God's dealings with his covenant people. Moses was a special man indeed: leader during the exodus; the first spokesman of the law; author of the primary writings. Moses was a central, pivotal character in their heritage. His place was lofty.

But our author was not trying to honor Moses as he wrote. He had something else in mind. He wanted his illustration to lead his weary readers to a higher insight, the insight that Jesus had a still harder task than Moses but handled that task so faithfully, so well indeed, that God gave him more honor than Moses received. Both served faithfully, but both could not receive the same glory.

That is what our writer sought to make plain—all for their encouragement. At his best, Moses remains a "secondary figure," a faithful servant *in* the family of God. But Jesus is a primary figure for our faith, positioned *over* the family now, and holding responsibility for it. In his faithfulness Moses guided a people. By his faithfulness—even dying for our sins—Jesus created a new people. No wonder the writer says that Jesus is "worthy of . . . more glory than Moses" (3:3).

III

Notice that phrase again: "worthy of much more glory." It
reminds us that Jesus ranks first in God's plan and in God's sight.
This word helps us wisely to recognize his lordship and stay in
our place. Like Moses, we are *in* the family, while Jesus stands,
by "divine right," *over* us there. Jesus was faithful. God has
made him our Lord, and he is forever worthy of our full trust and
highest honor.

In 1928 Allen Johnson edited a multivolumed dictionary of
American biography, the first of its kind in America. His
committee had problems while deciding basic restrictions about
entries. The group finally decided that no living persons would
be included in the dictionary, and that the work of any person
included would have been manifold in outreach. That planning
committee wanted to honor persons of extraordinary and
conspicuous accomplishment through services rendered,
persons whose work had increased insight and yielded
inspiration, the knowledge of whose lives could teach,
persuade, and encourage others. The published result was a
series of volumes to which many generations have been
indebted. [2]

Some lives *are* of unique dimension, and those who lived
those lives stand tall, worthy of honor in our thinking and our
regard. Moses was that kind of man. So were the prophets who
spoke for God, and the kings who lived wisely and ruled under
divine trust. So were some whom we have known and loved.

Jesus stands before us all with an unequaled honor, the writer
tells us. Although he is God's unique son, his greater glory is
attributed rather to his faithfulness. Jesus stands tall not only
because he is Son, but because of his unique work done in
faithfulness to the God who appointed him to it.

I thought of this while living abroad for a year, with the
Bavarian Alps in daily view. The jagged peaks rising here and

there impressed me deeply. They made me think of humans. Some persons rise to greater heights than others; and yet, however high any one may rise, he or she is but part of the rest of us. John Dewey once commented that "mountain peaks do not float unsupported; they do not even just rest upon the earth. They *are* the earth in one of its manifest operations." As with mountain peaks, so with humans. We all have the same beginning point and standing ground. Jesus elected to come where we live, begin where we begin, and experience what we experience. He soon rose higher than the rest of us—because he was faithful to God. His humanness was like yours and mine, his point of departure, but he did not let it be his horizon or his goal. There is a message here for us in our living, however trying, tempting, or troublesome our experiences and tasks may be.

IV

Make no mistake about it: life will test our faith and our fidelity—right down to the last. Some experiences will tempt us to disregard our divine "orders." Some experiences will tempt us to delay obeying our orders, or to leave them undone because of conflicts obedience to them might cause us. We must therefore prepare ourselves to honor God's trust of us. He has given us life, and he has trusted us with time, abilities, and opportunities. Let us each one rally the whole self to full obedience, leaving no part of the self unchecked or ungoverned.

Like Jesus, we too can match God's call with a ready obedience to his will. Faithfulness on our part is necessary. It is practical. It is possible. It happens when we inwardly agree to what God asks of us, and as we stand fully committed to please him at our productive best. This was the kind of faithfulness Jesus gave to God. And from that faithfulness our salvation was made possible.

SERMON STYLE 3. TOPICAL/DOCTRINAL

Death Did Not Win!

"O death, where is thy victory?
O death where is thy sting?"
. . . .
"O death, where is thy victory?
Therefore, my beloved brethren, be steadfast,
immovable, always abounding in the work
of the Lord, knowing that in the Lord
your labor is not in vain.
—I Cor. 15:55, 58

This is a strong and conclusive word. It closes out a lengthy message from Paul about what the resurrection of Christ means and foretells. Actually, all of I Corinthians 15 forms a sermon by itself. Paul must have used this message earlier somewhere. It is his doctrinal statement about how Jesus triumphed over death and what that victory means for our experience as persons who must die. Paul's statement is full. It is detailed, systematic, and appropriately illustrated. This message from Paul is so full of material that Martin Luther used no fewer than seventeen sermons to treat it. He spaced his sermons across nine months, preaching from August 1532 to April 1533.[3] I have only a few minutes with you today, so I will confine myself to the encouraging conclusion Paul gave his message.

After reminding the Corinthians about the fact of Jesus' resurrection, and after explaining the effects of that event upon all of life and death, Paul ended with an encouraging word to strengthen his readers for their daily tasks. As he summed up his message, Paul was saying that death did not win against Jesus and that it cannot win against those who belong to him. Death was not Jesus' undoing, and death will not undo his people.

I

Much like the people of our time, the Corinthians had been badgered by clashing notions about life and death. They knew the teaching of the Epicureans: "There is *nothing* after this life!" They had heard the word of the Stoics: "There is nothing *personal* after this life!" And they had heard the claim of the Platonists: "There is nothing but the *soul* after this life!" Paul countered all three notions in his message and labeled them false. Then he declared that there *is* something after this life, namely a full existence, and that we will be individual, personal, and in bodily form.

It is always heartening to remind ourselves that the grave is not the final scene of our existence, and that death does not have the last word about life. Cicero, filled with grief as he knelt in the cemetery and lit a taper at the tomb of his dead daughter Tullia, raised his voice in a question of lament: "Is this the quenching of thy life, O my daughter?" Our Christian answer is: No! The resurrection of Christ reassures us. We humans die, but we will live again. The resurrection of Christ reassures us of this.

II

The resurrection of Jesus also reminds us that our work is not lost when we die. Just as we have a future beyond death, so does the work we have done while on earth.

Death will not defeat us. The grave will not undo what we have done for God. We are therefore encouraged by Paul to "be steadfast" in our living and in our labors. Life has meaning and a future that death cannot defeat. God will give us that future "through our Lord Jesus Christ."

It is not easy to see that future during our troublesome moods. Our faith in it all is severely tested in precarious times, and when we fall victim to some disabling disease. It is not easy to see beyond death when we stand at the graveside of a friend or loved one whose life here was cut short by an incurable sickness or taken in a fatal accident. At such times we are tempted to accept the view before us, and the feelings within us, as the last word of life about itself. So often we are left with this incomplete word about life, which is a stark word about death, brokenness, sorrow, loss, and the indescribable horror of knowing that life is that way.

No, it is not easy to see the truth of our coming triumph when we feel at our lowest in mind and spirit. But the truth is still the truth and moods have nothing to do with it. What is true remains true, and the scenes of life cannot change it. The sorriest scene of human loss cannot long hinder the light that streams from the shining face of our resurrected Lord. Paul knew this! He had seen that shining face and was thus converted to preach the message he once tried to debunk and destroy. No wonder Paul became the man he now was! No wonder he wrote so fully about the resurrection truth! Paul had experienced the impact of that truth, and he knew its power to keep him steady in his life and labors.

You and I need steadiness as Christians today. Oh, how we need it, moved as some are by every wind of doctrine! The truth is still the truth, but we need to renew our faith in it so that we can go on serving that truth, go on building relationships in love, go on witnessing about God's grace, and go on blessing human lives. We must be steady in faith to go on being responsible and live to please God who seeks always to fulfill us.

The Christian message was given to help us handle our past, rightly shape the present, and keep us related to the future God has willed for us in Christ. This faith has a sure return because Christian life is an investment.

Death did not defeat Jesus. Death will not defeat us. Death could not win over Jesus. Death cannot win against those who

love and serve him. As Christians we do not live in vain, nor do
we work in vain.

III

Christian service is no vain or unpaid labor. We are saying
this to ourselves and others every time we have an epitaph carved
on a tombstone, every time we prepare a eulogy or condolence
honoring someone for his or her work. All of these references to
the impact of a life are more than mere nice words for a hard
time. We know that there is meaning in work nobly done, work
done in faith and love. We know that labor has meaning that
should last and multiply in effects. We also know that labor
should be rewarded.

The New Testament promises that it will be. There is a
history of harvests here on this side of death, and there is a
harvest on the other side as well. We need not fear being hurt or
discouraged by having what we have done rejected as of no
worth, and consequently going unpaid. The text promises
returns from our work for God. It promises wages to match
services rendered. With this kind of future in view, Paul has
encouraged us to "Keep on keeping on!" History here must not
daunt us, and death must not frighten us. Death will not be our
undoing, nor shall we be disappointed by God.

IV

The text therefore helps us to increase our steadfastness in
faith and faithfulness in work for God. Every Christian is
reminded that there is a future to what we are and returns from
what we do. It is a good future, a future with eternal returns
shared with us by a loving and gracious God. No Christian will
have believed and lived and served in vain. No effort for Christ
will fall flat in defeat.

Here again is the text. Let it warm your heart with hope:

> "O death, where is thy victory?
> O death, where is thy sting?"
> . . . .
> Therefore, my beloved brethren,
> be steadfast, immovable, always
> abounding in the work of the Lord,
> knowing that in the Lord your labor
> is not in vain.

NOTES

PREFACE
1. *Roman Society and Roman Law in the New Testament* (Oxford: At the University Press, 1963), from the preface.

CHAPTER I: The Sermon in Context

1. "Preacher," in *This Ministry: The Contribution of Henry Sloane Coffin* (New York: Scribner's, 1946), p. 59.
2. *Faith and Its Psychology*, Studies in Theology (London: Duckworth, 1909), p. 18.
3. *The Evangelical Faith*, trans. Geoffrey W. Bromiley. (Grand Rapids: Eerdmans, 1974), 1:196.
4. See Alfred McBride, *Catechetics: A Theology of Proclamation* (Milwaukee: Bruce Publishing Company, 1966), p. 122.
5. G. C. Berkouwer, *Sin*, trans. Philip C. Holtrop, Studies in Dogmatics (Grand Rapids: Eerdmans, 1971), p. 189.
6. See Sangster's *Craft of Sermon Illustration* (Philadelphia: Westminster Press, 1950), pp. 24-25.
7. On these, see my *Responsible Pulpit* (Anderson: Warner Press, 1974), esp. pp. 108-10; Henry H. Mitchell, *Black Preaching* (Philadelphia: Lippincott, 1970), esp. pp. 188-95.
8. One of the most instructive manuals on shaping an effective sermon design is the study of H. Grady Davis, *Design for Preaching* (Philadelphia: Muhlenberg Press, 1958). Two other additionally helpful studies are: Milton Crum, Jr., *Manual on Preaching: A New Process of Sermon Development* (Valley Forge: Judson Press, 1977) and Henry H. Mitchell, *The Recovery of Preaching* (Yale Lyman Beecher Lectures, 1974) (New York and San Francisco: Harper, 1977).
9. Sermons in *The Twentieth Century Pulpit*, ed. James W. Cox (Nashville: Abingdon, 1978), by, respectively, Billy Graham, pp. 64-74; Harry Emerson Fosdick, pp. 57-63 (see also "Death Did Not Win!" in chapter 7 of this book); Edmund A. Steimle, 220-25; Fulton John Sheen, pp. 202-6.

10. Andrew W. Blackwood, *The Preparation of Sermons* (Nashville and New York: Abingdon-Cokesbury Press, 1948), p. 101.

11. The complete sermon is taken from Barth's *Deliverance to the Captives* (London: SCM Press, 1961) and reproduced in Cox, *The Twentieth Century Pulpit*, pp. 15-19.

12. Clyde E. Fant, Jr., and William M. Pinson, Jr., *Twenty Centuries of Great Preaching* (Waco, Tex.: Word Books, 1971) 10:100.

13. See James W. Cox, *The Twentieth Century Pulpit*, pp. 9-14.

14. *Ibid.*, pp. 197-201.

15. *The Craft of Sermon Construction* (Philadelphia: Westminster Press, 1951), p. 31. For Sangster's treatment of these three classifications, see pp. 29-118.

16. H. C. Brown, Jr.; H. Gordon Clinard; and Jesse J. Northcutt, *Steps to the Sermon: A Plan for Sermon Preparation* (Nashville: Broadman, 1963), p. 137.

17. See Everett M. Rogers and Dilip K. Bhowmik, "Homophily-Heterophily: Relational Concepts for Communication Research," in *Speech Communication Behavior: Perspectives and Principles*, ed. Larry L. Barker, and Robert J. Kibler (Englewood Cliffs, N.J.: Prentice-Hall, 1971).

18. *The Mystery of Preaching* (London: James Clarke and Co., 1934), p. 37.

19. See Gerald S. Sloyan, *Worship in a New Key* (New York: Herder and Herder, 1965), esp. pp. 57-61.

20. *The Shape of the Gospel: Interpreting the Bible Through the Christian Year* (Nashville: Abingdon, 1970), p. 7. On the relation of preaching to the liturgy and lectionary, see also Crum, *Manual on Preaching*, pp. 127-44, and an earlier discussion by Donald Macleod, *Word and Sacrament: A Preface to Preaching* (Englewood Cliffs, N.J.: Prentice-Hall, 1960), esp. chaps. 5 and 7.

21. (New York: Harper, 1963).

22. *Ibid.*, p. 157. For an appreciation and critique of Bonhoeffer as preacher, see Fant and Pinson, *Twenty Centuries of Great Preaching*, 12:91-137.

23. *Treasure in Earthen Vessels: The Church as a Human Community* (New York: Harper, 1961), p. 64.

24. See Stephen Crites, "The Narrative Quality of Experience," *Journal of the American Academy of Religion*, September 1971, pp. 291-311; Harald Weinrich, "Narrative Theology," *The Crisis of Religious Language*, ed. Johann B. Metz and Jean-Pierre Jossua, trans. Francis McDonagh, Concilium Series (New York: Herder and Herder, 1973), pp. 46-56.

25. Mitchell, *The Recovery of Preaching*. See note 8.

26. "The Successful Minister," in Walter P. Doe, ed., *Eminent Authors on Effective Revival Preaching* (Providence, R.I.: Greene, 1876), p. 124.

27. See Cox, *The Twentieth Century Pulpit*, pp. 15-19.

28. *Lectures to My Students*, one-volume edition (Grand Rapids: Baker Book House, 1977), p. 72.

CHAPTER II: Designing the Narrative/Story Sermon

1. See Gerhard von Rad, *Old Testament Theology*, vol. I (New York and Evanston: Harper, 1962), p. 121. Trans. D. M. G. Stalker. See also pp. 105-28 for the fuller discussion.

2. On this genre of literature, see Jay A. Wilcoxen, "Narrative," in John H. Hayes, ed., *Old Testament Form Criticism* (San Antonio: Trinity University Press, 1974), esp. pp. 57-98. See also R. Scholes and R. Kellogg, *The Nature of Narrative* (London: Oxford University Press, 1966).

3. For a suggested distinction between "story" and "history" see James Barr, "Story and History in Biblical Theology," in *The Journal of Religion*, January 1976, esp. pp. 5-11.

4. See James A. Sanders, *Torah and Canon* (Philadelphia: Fortress Press, 1972), esp. pp. 15-20. Sanders cites I. Sam. 12:7-9 as the classic summary regarding the saving deeds of God in Israel's life. "In that one verse the essence of what is recorded in far fuller compass in the Books of Genesis through Joshua is recited" (p. 17).

5. See Wesley Kort, *Narrative Elements and Religious Meanings* (Philadelphia: Fortress Press, 1975). Kort distinguishes four narrative elements of importance: atmosphere, character, plot, and tone. His discussion relates to modern novels but the insights are helpful for our examination of scripture narratives.

6. James H. Cone, *God of the Oppressed* (New York: Seabury Press, Crossroads Book, 1975), p. 57. See also pp. 58-60, 102-7.

7. See James W. English, *Handyman of the Lord: The Life and Ministry of the Reverend William Holmes Borders* (New York: Meredith Press, 1967), esp. pp. 3-8.

8. *Road Without Turning: The Story of Reverend James H. Robinson, An Autobiography* (New York: Farrar, Straus, 1950), pp. 60, 61.

9. On this distinction, see Hans Frei, *The Eclipse of Biblical Narrative* (New Haven: Yale University Press, 1974), esp. pp. 10-16. See also Leo Braudy, *Narrative Form in History and Fiction* (Princeton: Princeton University Press, 1970); Maurice Mandelbaum, "A Note on History as Narrative," in *History and Theology*, 6 (1967), pp. 413-19, and the responses of W. H. Dray, R. G. Ely, R. Gruner, "Mandelbaum on History as Narrative: A Discussion," in *History and Theory*, 8 (1969), pp. 275-94.

10. *The Scottish Pulpit: From the Reformation to the Present Day* (London: Charles Burnet and Co., 1887), p. 174. See also Jean L. Watson, *Life of Andrew Thomson*, p. 82.

11. The affirmational proposition is there even if the translation is made in terms of an adverbial expression: "When God began to create heaven and earth." See the discussion of the options (against the background of the similar Babylonian *Enuma Elish*) in Alexander Heidel, *The Babylonian Genesis: The Story of Creation* (Chicago: University of Chicago, Phoenix Books, 1963), esp. pp. 92 ff. See also *(contra)*, Edward J. Young, *Studies in Genesis One* (Philadelphia: Presbyterian and Reformed Publishing Company, 1964), esp. pp. 1-14; and Bernhard W. Anderson, *Creation Versus Chaos* (New York: Association Press, 1967), esp. pp. 17-42.

12. Tractate *Pesahim* 10:5. *The Mishnah*, trans. Herbert Danby (London: Oxford University Press, 1933), p. 151.

13. See his *Die Schrift und ihre Verdeutschung*, with Franz Rosenzweig (Berlin: Schocken Verlag, 1936), p. 56.

14. On this see Joachim Jeremias, *The Parables of Jesus*, trans. S. H. Hooke (New York: Scribner's, 1963), esp. pp. 113-14; and *New Testament Theology: The Proclamation of Jesus*, trans. John Bowden (Scribner's, 1971), esp. pp. 1-37; Matthew Black, *An Aramaic Approach to the Gospels and Acts*, 3rd ed. (Oxford: Clarendon Press, 1967), esp. pp. 156-85.

15. *My Lord, What a Morning: An Autobiography* (New York: Viking Press, 1956), pp. 9-10.

16. For one of the helpful treatments for doing this kind of study, see William F. Irmscher, *The Nature of Literature* (New York: Holt, Rinehart, and Winston, 1975) and Wesley Kort, *Narrative Elements and Religious Meanings* (see note 5, this chapter).

17. "The Use of Biblical Narrative in Expository Preaching," *The Asbury Seminarian*, July 1979, p. 14

18. See Cox, *The Twentieth Century Pulpit*, pp. 141-52.

19. See the appreciation and critique of Marshall as preacher in Fant and Pinson, *Twenty Centuries of Great Preaching*, 12:3-10.

20. See Cox, *The Twentieth Century Pulpit*, pp. 64-74.

21. See *Best Sermons: 1959–1960 Protestant Edition*, vol. 7, ed. G. Paul Butler (New York: Thomas Y. Crowell, 1959), pp. 228-34.

22. (New York: Harper, 1948).

23. (New York: Harper, 1963), pp. 127-34.

24. See Fant and Pinson, *Twenty Centuries of Great Preaching*, 8:184-96.

25. On which, see John Charles Cooper, *Fantasy and the Human Spirit* (Philadelphia: Pilgrim Press, 1975).

26. *Lectures on Preaching* (New York: Dutton, 1877), p. 19.

CHAPTER III: Designing the Textual/Expository Sermon

1. Dwight E. Stevenson, *In the Biblical Preacher's Workshop* (Nashville: Abingdon, 1967), p. 146.

2. *What to Preach* (New York: George H. Doran Co., 1926), p. 42.

3. *Biblical Exegesis in the Apostolic Period* (Grand Rapids: Eerdmans, 1975), esp. pp. 79-132, 158-85, 205-20. See also F. F. Bruce, *New Testament Development of Old Testament Themes* (Eerdmans, 1968).

4. For an excellent translation of *On Christian Doctrine*, see D. W. Robertson, ed., trans. (New York: Library of Liberal Arts, 1958). On Augustine as preacher, see *The Preaching of Augustine*, ed. Jaroslav Pelikan, trans. Francine Cardman (Philadelphia: Fortress Press, 1973), esp. pp. vii-xxi.

5. (Philadelphia: Fortress Press, 1965). English trans. by Karl E. Mattson.

6. On the subject of abstraction, as I use it here, see the discussion in *Dictionary of Philosophy and Psychology*, ed. James Mark Baldwin (New York: Macmillan, 1901), 1:6.

7. On this matter of document-texts, see Edward W. Said, *Beginnings: Intention and Method* (New York: Basic Books, 1975), esp. pp. 191-275.

8. On the categorical descriptions of "statements," "expressions," and "prescriptives," see Anders Jeffner, *The Study of Religious Language* (London: SCM Press, 1972), esp. pp. 11-12, 68-104; and J. L. Austin, *How to Do Things with Words*, ed. J. O. Urmson (New York: Oxford University Press, Galaxy

Books, 1965); and John Wilson, *Language and the Pursuit of Truth* (Cambridge:.At the University Press, 1960), esp. pp. 47-74.

9. The writings of Paul are filled with imperatives. On the relation between the imperative and the indicative, see Rudolf Bultmann, *The Theology of the New Testament*, vol. 1, trans. Kendrick Grobel. New York: Scribner's, 1951), esp. pp. 332-33, 338-39. Instances of the imperative in the Old Testament (in law, exhortation, promise, etc.), see James Muilenburg, *The Way of Israel: Biblical Faith and Ethics* (New York: Harper, 1961), esp. pp. 18-30, 74-98.

10. *Preaching the Word of God* (New York: Scribner's, 1943), p. 7.

11. Stevenson, *In the Biblical Preacher's Workshop*, p. 61.

12. *Ibid.*, p. 62. For his studies promoting a sermon on an entire book of the Bible, see his *Preaching on the Books of the New Testament* (New York: Harper, 1956) and *Preaching on the Books of the Old Testament* (Harper, 1961).

13. Cox, *The Twentieth Century Pulpit*, p. 64.

14. *The Soul of Frederick W. Robertson: The Brighton Preacher* (New York: Harper, 1947), p. 50.

15. For an appreciative critique of Robertson's preaching and ministry, see *The Preaching of F. W. Robertson*, ed. Gilbert E. Doan, Jr., in the Preacher's Paperback Library (Philadelphia: Fortress Press, 1964), esp. pp. 11-73. See also J. R. Blackwood, *The Soul of Frederick W. Robertson*, chap. 9 ("The Groundwork of the Sermon") and chap. 10 ("The Art of Preaching").

16. *Princes of the Church* (London: Hodder and Stoughton, 1921), p. 249. Interestingly, Nicoll said that Maclaren never desired to publish, and that it was only after strong urging from him that those now famous *Expositions of Holy Scripture* were done.

17. An excellent self-evaluation instrument to test the quality of your own expository attempts is found in an article by James W. Cox, "How Good Is Your Expository Preaching?" *The Pulpit Digest*, November-December 1979, pp. 45-48. The self-test involves answering twelve questions, all annotated to assist understanding and use of them. A much larger and detailed volume of help from Cox is his *Guide to Biblical Preaching* (Nashville: Abingdon, 1976).

18. Geoffrey Skelton, *Paul Hindemith: The Man Behind the Music: A Biography* (London: Victor Gollancz, 1975), p. 15.

CHAPTER IV: Designing the Doctrinal/Topical Sermon

1. See Gerald E. Knoff, "The Churches Expect a Teaching Ministry," in *The Minister and Christian Nurture*, ed. Nathaniel F. Forsyth (Nashville: Abingdon, 1957), pp. 9-26. Knoff discusses the teaching ministry against the backgrounds of Judaic rabbinical circles, the Protestant Reformation, and in the later traditions of several major denominations. See also James D. Smart, *The Teaching Ministry of the Church* (Philadelphia: Westminster Press, 1954), esp. pp. 13-19; and Robert C. Worley, *Preaching and Teaching in the Earliest Church* (Philadelphia: Westminster Press, 1967), esp. pp. 30-86. See also Floyd V. Filson, "The Christian Teacher in the First Century," *Journal of Biblical Literature*, 1941, pp. 317-28.

2. *What to Preach*, p. 13.

3. For example, see Rom. 6:17-18; Phil. 4:8-9; Titus 2:1-8; and II Pet. 1:2-8 especially.

4. For a discussion of the Sermon on the Mount as a focal instance of how Jesus blended preaching and teaching, proclaiming as he taught, instructing as he invited, see my *Responsible Pulpit*, pp. 93-100.

5. Donald M. Baillie, *The Theology of the Sacraments: and Other Papers* (London: Faber and Faber, 1964), pp. 141-42.

6. *Positive Preaching and Modern Mind* (London: Hodder and Stoughton, 1907), p. 5.

7. For a profitable study of the chief New Testament passages that speak directly of "doctrine," see the list in Robert Young, *Analytical Concordance to the Bible*, p. 2671, columns a/b. Although the renderings offered for each word are my own, an examination of the relevant passages (in both the Old and New Testament) will help the reader to see the basis for the renderings. Additional lexical insight appears (for N.T. terms) in Kittel's *Theological Dictionary of the New Testament*, 10 vols. (Grand Rapids: Eerdmans, 1964–76); for O.T. terms, see William L. Holladay, ed., *A Concise Hebrew and Aramaic Lexicon of the Old Testment* (Eerdmans, 1971), and *Theological Dictionary of the Old Testament*, ed. G. Johannes Botterweck and Helmer Ringgren, trans. John T. Willis, Geoffrey Bromiley, David E. Green, successive volumes appearing (Eerdmans, 1974–).

8. *The Craft of Sermon Construction*, p. 45.

9. *Freedom for Ministry: A Critical Affirmation of the Church and Its Mission* (New York and San Francisco: Harper, 1979), p. 178.

10. A. W. W. Dale, *The Life of R. W. Dale of Birmingham* (London: Hodder and Stoughton, 1898), p. 107.

11. Neuhaus, *Freedom for Ministry*, p. 174.

12. Paul S. Rees, editorial, "Uncomfortable Questions," *The Herald* magazine, October 31, 1962, p. 2.

13. In Cox, *The Twentieth Century Pulpit*, pp. 9-14.

14. *Ibid.*, pp. 75-81.

15. *Ibid.*, pp. 108-14.

16. *Ibid.*, pp. 237-41.

17. See Alexander Whyte, *With Mercy and with Judgment* (London: Hodder and Stoughton, n.d.), pp. 269-70. See also Whyte's *Thirteen Appreciations* (Edinburgh and London: Oliphant, Anderson and Ferrier, n.d.), pp. 278, 280.

18. Arthur John Gossip, "The Whole Counsel of God: The Place of Biblical Doctrine in Preaching," *Interpretation*, July 1947, p. 327.

CHAPTER V: Designing the Funeral Sermon

1. Howard Thurman, *Footprints of a Dream: The Story of the Church for the Fellowship of All Peoples* (New York: Harper, 1959), pp. 15-16, 18.

2. See William F. Hatcher, *John Jasper: The Unmatched Negro Philosopher and Preacher* (New York: Fleming H. Revell, 1908), p. 38.

3. *Ibid.*, p. 175. There is a new and revised version of these sermons as prepared by Clyde E. Fant, Jr., and W. M. Pinson, Jr., for their treatment of Jasper's work in their multi-volume study, *Twenty Centuries of Great*

Preaching. See 4:237. The revised version of the sermon has modernized the dialect-spelling for those who are not familiar with it.

4. For the text of the eulogy, see Benjamin E. Mays, *Born to Rebel: An Autobiography by Benjamin E. Mays* (New York: Scribner's, 1971), pp. 357-60.

5. James Baldwin, *Notes of a Native Son* (Boston: Beacon Press, 1955), p. 105.

6. See David Dempsey, "The Dying Speak for Themselves on a TV Special," *New York Times,* Sunday, April 25, 1976, Section 2.

7. *Meditations of the Heart* (New York: Harper, 1953), p. 142. The italics are Thurman's.

CHAPTER VI: Studying the Methods of Master Preachers

1. *The Preparation of Sermons,* p. 18.

2. An alphabetical listing of the preachers treated appears in 13:359-60.

3. For a survey and appreciation covering the period 1871 (the founding year of the lectureship) through 1950, see Edgar DeWitt Jones, *The Royalty of the Pulpit* (New York: Harper, 1951). The lecturers and lecture titles are listed on pp. 432-36.

The lecturers and lecture titles through 1974 are listed by Ralph G. Turnbull, in his *History of Preaching,* (Grand Rapids: Baker Book House, 1974), 3:533-36.

4. For a listing from the first lectures in 1921 down through 1973, see *ibid.,* 3:537-38.

5. (London: SCM Press, 1963).

6. See Martin Luther King, Jr., *Strength to Love,* pp. 108-17.

7. Blackwood, *The Preparation of Sermons,* p. 23.

8. Phillips Brooks, *Lectures on Preaching,* p. 5.

9. *Sermons Preached in a University Church* (Nashville: Abingdon, 1959), p. 9.

10. On the matter of an economical use of words in the pulpit, see my *Sermon in Perspective: A Study of Communication and Charisma* (Grand Rapids: Baker Book House, 1976), esp. pp. 95-99.

11. John Henry Jowett, *The Preacher: His Life and Work* (New York: Harper, 1912), p. 127.

12. *How Shall They Preach* (Elgin, Ill.: Progressive Baptist Publishing House, 1977), p. 63-64.

13. *Ibid.,* see pp. 64-65.

14. In addition to single sermons published in preachers' magazines across the years, there is now a collection of sermons, published as part of his Beecher Lectures at Yale in 1976. See pp. 97-148 of *How Shall They Preach.*

The student should not miss the opportunity to hear Gardner Taylor via the many tape recordings from religious radio programs, NCCCUSA-sponsored, on which he has spoken across the years: "The Art of Living," October 1969–April 1970; "National Radio Pulpit," July–September 1959. Copies of the sermons are available through Reigner Recording Library, Union Theological Seminary, Richmond, Virginia.

15. See his *Sermons Preached at Brighton* (New York: Harper, n.d.), pp. 300-307.

16. Joseph Fort Newton, *The Angel in the Soul* (New York: Harper, 1932), pp. 15-24.

17. Robertson, *Sermons Preached at Brighton*, pp. 404-15; Weatherhead, *The Autobiography of Jesus* (Nashville: Abingdon Festival Books, 1980), pp. 37-49.

18. See Alexander Whyte, *With Mercy and With Judgment* (New York: George H. Doran Co., n.d.), pp. 240-49; *Favorite Sermons of John A. Broadus*, ed. Vernon Latrelle Stanfield (New York: Harper, 1959), pp. 28-37.

19. Jowett, in *Great Gospel Sermons* (New York: Fleming H. Revell, 1949), 1:193-201; Macartney, *The Greatest Texts of the Bible* (Nashville: Abingdon-Cokesbury Press, 1947), pp. 84-96.

20. Macartney, *Salute Thy Soul* (Nashville: Abingdon, 1957), pp. 34-43.

21. See *Best Sermons*, 1947–48 ed., ed. G. Paul Butler (New York: Harper, 1947), pp. 85-91.

22. See his *Encounter with Spurgeon*, trans. John W. Doberstein (Philadelphia: Fortress Press, 1963), p. 45.

23. *Pulpit Giants: What Made Them Great* (Chicago: Moody Press, 1973), pp. 165-74.

CHAPTER VII: Three Illustrated Designs

1. See his "Preaching the Whole Gospel," in *Preaching in These Times*, by Buttrick, Tittle, Bradford, *et al.* (New York: Scribner's, 1940), p. 12.

2. *Dictionary of American Biography* (New York: Scribner's, 1928).

3. See *Luther's Works*, vol. 28, ed. Hilton C. Oswald (St. Louis: Concordia Publishing House, 1973).

FOR FURTHER READING

CHAPTER I: The Sermon in Context

Abbey, Merrill R. *The Shape of the Gospel: Interpreting the Bible Through the Christian Year*. Nashville: Abingdon Press, 1970.
_____. *Communication in Pulpit and Parish*. Philadelphia: Westminster Press, 1973.
Baumann, J. David. *An Introduction to Contemporary Preaching*. Grand Rapids: Baker Book House, 1972.
Broadus, John A. *On the Preparation and Delivery of Sermons*. 4th ed., rev. by Vernon L. Stanfield. New York and San Francisco: Harper and Row, 1979.
Fant, Clyde E. *Preaching for Today*. New York: Harper, 1977.
Luccock, Halford E. *In the Minister's Workshop*. Nashville and New York: Abingdon-Cokesbury Press, 1944.
Massey, James Earl. *The Sermon in Perspective: A Study of Communication and Charisma*. Grand Rapids: Baker Book House, 1976.
Ornstein, Robert E. *The Psychology of Consciousness*, 2nd ed. New York: Harcourt, Brace, Jovanovich, 1977.
Pennington, Chester. *God Has a Communication Problem: Creative Preaching Today*. New York: Hawthorn Books, 1976.
Read, David H. C. *Sent from God*. Nashville: Abingdon Press, 1974.
Steimle, Edmund A. *Preaching the Story*. Philadelphia: Fortress Press, 1979.
Thompson, William D., and Bennett, Gordon C. *Dialogue Preaching*. Valley Forge: Judson Press, 1969.

Welsh, Clement. *Preaching in a New Key*. Philadelphia: United Church Press, 1974.

CHAPTER II: Designing the Narrative/Story Sermon

Achtemeier, Elizabeth. *Creative Preaching: Finding the Words*. Nashville: Abingdon, 1980.
Hall, Thor. *The Future Shape of Preaching*. Philadelphia: Fortress Press, 1971.
Killinger, John, ed. *Experimental Preaching*. Nashville: Abingdon Press, 1973.
Mitchell, Henry H. *Black Preaching*. New York: Harper Paperbacks, 1979.
_____. *The Recovery of Preaching*. New York and San Francisco: Harper, 1977.
Wiggins, James B., ed. *Religion as Story*. New York and Evanston: Harper, 1975.

CHAPTER III: Designing the Textual/Expository Sermon

Best, Ernest. *From Text to Sermon*. Atlanta: John Knox Press, 1978.
Cox, James W. *A Guide to Biblical Preaching*. Nashville: Abingdon, 1976.
Stevenson, Dwight E. *In the Biblical Preacher's Workshop*. Nashville: Abingdon Press, 1967.

CHAPTER IV: Designing the Doctrinal/Topical Sermon

Abbey, Merrill R. *Living Doctrine in a Vital Pulpit*. Nashville: Abingdon Press, 1964.
Barr, James. *The Bible in the Modern World*. Naperville, Ill.: Allenson paperback, 1977.
Blackwood, Andrew W. *Doctrinal Preaching for Today*. Nashville: Abingdon Press, 1956.
Bruce, F. F. *Tradition Old and New*. Grand Rapids: Zondervan, 1970.
Ebeling, Gerhard. *The Word of God and Tradition*. Philadelphia: Fortress Press, 1968. English trans. by S. H. Hooke.
Henry, Carl F.H., ed. *Basic Christian Doctrines*. New York: Holt, Rinehart and Winston, 1962.

Kelly, J. N. D. *Early Christian Doctrines*. Rev. ed. New York: Harper, 1977.

Mounce, Robert H. *The Essential Nature of New Testament Preaching*. Grand Rapids: Eerdmans, 1960.

Pelikan, Jaroslav. *Historical Theology: Continuity and Change in Christian Doctrine*. New York: Corpus Instrumentorum, 1971.

Worley, Robert C. *Preaching and Teaching in the Earliest Church*. Philadelphia: Westminster Press, 1967.

CHAPTER V: Designing the Funeral Sermon

Allen, R. Earl. *Funeral Source Book*. Grand Rapids: Baker Book House, 1974 paperback ed. of 1964 release.

Bailey, Lloyd R., Sr. *Biblical Perspectives on Death*. Philadelphia: Fortress Press, 1978.

Daniels, Earl. *The Funeral Message: Its Preparation and Significance*. Nashville: Cokesbury Press, 1937.

Gorer, Geoffrey. *Death, Grief and Mourning*. New York: Arno Press, 1977 reprint of 1965 ed.

Grollman, Earl A., ed. *Concerning Death: A Practical Guide for the Living*. Boston: Beacon Press, 1964.

Hollingsworth, Charles E., and Pasnau, Robert O. *The Family in Mourning*. New York: Grune and Stratton, 1977.

Irion, Paul E. *The Funeral: Vestige or Value?* Nashville: Abingdon Press, 1966.

Jackson, Edgar N. *The Christian Funeral: Its Meaning, Its Purpose, and Its Modern Practice*. New York: Channel Press, 1966.

Poovey, W. A. *Planning a Christian Funeral: A Minister's Guide*. Minneapolis: Augsburg Publishing House, 1978.

Scott, Nathan A., Jr., ed. *The Modern Vision of Death*. Richmond, Va.: John Knox Press, 1967.

Wallis, Charles L., ed. *The Funeral Encyclopedia: A Source Book*. New York: Baker Books paperback, 1973.

CHAPTER VI. Studying the Methods of Master Preachers

Boddie, Charles Emerson. *God's "Bad Boys": Eight Outstanding Black Preachers*. Valley Forge: Judson Press, 1972.

Butler, G. Paul, ed. *Best Sermons*. Successive publications beginning in 1943-44, but especially vol. 7 (1959–60), New York: Thomas Y.

Crowell Company, 1959; and vol. 8 (1962), New York and
  Princeton: Van Nostrand, 1962.
Cox, James W., ed. *The Twentieth Century Pulpit*. Nashville:
  Abingdon, 1978.
Demaray, Donald E. *Pulpit Giants: What Made Them Great*.
  Chicago: Moody Press, 1973.
Fant, Clyde E., Jr., and Pinson, William M. Jr., eds. *Twenty
  Centuries of Great Preaching: An Encyclopedia of Preaching*.
  Thirteen volumes. Waco: Word Books, 1971.
Gammie, Alexander. *Preachers I Have Heard*. London: Pickering and
  Inglis, 1945.
Holland, DeWitte. *The Preaching Tradition: A Brief History*.
  Nashville: Abingdon, 1980.
Homiletic: Review of Publications in Religious Communication. 3510
  Woodley Road N.W. Washington, D.C. 20016.
Hoard, Walter B., ed. *Outstanding Black Sermons*, vol. 2. Valley
  Forge: Judson Press, 1979.
Macleod, Donald, ed. *Here Is My Method: The Art of Sermon
  Construction*. Westwood, N.J.: Fleming H. Revell, 1952.
Roddy, Clarence Stonelynn, ed. *We Prepare and Preach: The Practice
  of Sermon Construction and Delivery*. Chicago: Moody Press, 1959.
Wiersbe, Warren. *Walking with the Giants: A Minister's Guide to
  Good Reading and Great Preaching*. Grand Rapids: Baker Book
  House, 1976.

INDEX

Abbey, Merrill R., 26, 27
Anderson, Marian, 45-46
Athanasius, 51
Augustine, 51

Baillie, Donald M., 22, 62, 69-71
Baldwin, James, 80-81
Barnhouse, Donald Grey, 52
Barth, Karl, 22, 32
Black church tradition, 37-38, 39, 79
Black, James, 25
Blackwood, Andrew W., 83, 86
Blackwood, James R., 57
Boice, James W., 52
Bonhoeffer, Dietrich, 27, 28
Borders, Williams Holmes, 37, 38, 39
Boreham, F. W., 48, 90
Bowie, Walter Russell, 15
Boyd, Archibald, 57
Brahms, Johannes, 24
Brief History of Preaching, A (Brilioth), 51
Brilioth, Yngve, 51-52
British Weekly, The, 58
Broadus, John Albert, 92
Brooks, Phillips, 49, 86

Brown, Charles Reynolds, 52
Buber, Martin, 42
Butler, Bishop Joseph, 73
Buttrick, George Arthur, 52, 86, 102

Child, C. M., 19
Cicero, 108
Coffin, Henry Sloane, 51, 61
Communication theory, 24-25
Communion of Saints, The (Bonhoeffer), 27
Cone, James H., 37, 39
Constitution on the Sacred Liturgy, The, 26
Cox, James W., 11
Craft of Sermon Construction, The (Sangster), 23
Curzon, Clifford, 31
Cuyler, T. L., 32

Dale, A. W. W., 64
Dale, R. W., 64-65, 68, 89
Dargan, Edwin C., 85
Davies, Horton, 85
Demaray, Donald E., 95
Design, sermon
    contemporary approaches, 24-30

Design, sermon (*continued*)
  forms, 20-24, 43-48, 52-60, 65-73
  general principles, 30-34
  goals, 18-20
  special principles, 43-48, 52-60,
    65-73, 76-82
Dewey, John, 106

Emerson, Ralph Waldo, 45

Fant, Clyde E., Jr., 11, 84
Forsyth, P. T., 63

Gamaliel, Rabban, II, 41
Gossip, Arthur John, 73, 90
Graham, Billy, 48, 56-57
Guinn, G. Earl, 71-72
Gustafson, James M., 28

Haley, Alex, 48
Hankey, Katherine, 42
Haywood, Jim, 38
Hindemith, Paul, 60
Hines, Samuel G., 52
History of Preaching, A (Dargan), 85

Inge, W. R., 15

James, John Angell, 68
Jasper, John, 78-79
Johnson, Allen, 105
Jowett, John Henry, 89, 92

Kaiser, Walter C., Jr., 46, 47
Killinger, John, 72
King, Martin Luther, Jr., 48, 80, 85

Longenecker, Richard W., 51
Lost Gospel, The (Luccock), 48
Luccock, Robert E., 48
Luther, Martin, 107
Lyman Beecher Lectures, 40, 49, 85,
    90

Macartney, Clarence Edward, 92

Maclaren, Alexander, 57
Marshall, Peter, 47-48
Masefield, John, 87
Mays, Benjamin E., 80
Meyer, F. B., 52
Mitchell, Henry H., 29
Morgan, G. Campbell, 52

Narrative sermons. *See* Story
Neuhaus, Richard John, 64, 66
Newton, Joseph Fort, 91
Nicoll, W. Robertson, 57-58
Noyes, Morgan Phelps, 55

Ockenga, Harold John, 52
On Christian Doctrine (Augustine),
    51
Origen, 51

Pinson, William M., 11, 84
Pulpit Giants (Demaray), 95

Rad, Gerhard von, 35
Ray, Sandy F., 52
Rees, Paul S., 52, 67
Robertson, Frederick W., 57, 91-92
Robinson, James Herman, 38, 39

Sangster, W. E., 19, 23, 64
Scherer, Paul, 90
Schnabel, Artur, 31
Schweizer, Eduard, 22
Scripture passage
  context, 31-32
  focus, 31
  layout, 31
  message, 31-32
  natural divisions, 31
Sermon, the
  and church year, 26
  and liturgy, 26-28, 86-87
  application of, 32-33
  arrangement of, 29-30
  as abstraction of text, 52
  climax of impression, 20

communication process in, 24-25
concern oriented, 15-16, 25
conclusion to, 33
design of, 20-24, 43-48, 52-60,
    65-73
doctrinal, 61-74
expository, 50-60
funeral, 75-82
how to study, 83-96
idea, 30-33
introduction, 33
narrative (story), 35-37, 38-42,
    43-49
order and movement in, 32
"points," 32
structure, 31-32
textual, 52-60
topical, 65-74
writing, 33
Sherwin-White, A. N., 12
Spurgeon, Charles Haddon, 33, 94-
    95
Stevenson, Dwight E., 50, 56
Stewart, James S., 52
Story (or narrative),
    appeal of, 28-29, 35, 37-38, 39-41
    as scriptural mode, 35-37
    design for preaching, 43-48

in black church, 37-38
in human experience, 39-42, 48-
    49
in Jesus' preaching, 40, 42-43
teaching power of, 43-45
Stott, John R. W., 72
Strength to Love (King), 48

Taylor, Gardner C., 90
Taylor, W. M., 40
Thielicke, Helmut, 16, 85, 94-95
Thompson, William D., 12
Thomson, Andrew, 40
Thurman, Howard, 78, 82
Turnbull, Ralph G., 85
Twenty Centuries of Great Preaching
    (Fant and Pinson), 11, 84

Varieties of English Preaching
    (Davies), 85

Wagner, Richard, 24
Warrack Lectures, 51, 85
Weatherhead, Leslie D., 92-93
Whyte, Alexander, 73, 92
Whyte, Robert B., 92
Woodyard, David O., 48